AN OXFORD
COLLEGE
AT WAR

HARRIET PATRICK

AN OXFORD COLLEGE AT WAR

CORPUS CHRISTI COLLEGE, 1914–18

PROFILE
EDITIONS

First published in Great Britain in 2018 by
Profile Editions, an imprint of
PROFILE BOOKS LTD
3 Holford Yard
Bevin Way
London WC1X 9HD
www.profileeditions.com

10 9 8 7 6 5 4 3 2 1

Typeset in Sabon by MacGuru Ltd
Printed and bound in Great Britain by Clays Ltd, Elcograf S.p.A.

ISBN 978 1 78125 821 7
eISBN 978 1 90899 072 3

FSC
www.fsc.org
MIX
Paper from
responsible sources
FSC® C018072

CONTENTS

Afterword: Corpus After the Armistice 93

PREFACE

This publication focuses on how the First World War affected Corpus directly: there is not space here to discuss the broader impact of the war, or to venture far outside the College. Furthermore, this wartime history is limited by what records have been preserved in Corpus Archives. While there is a wealth of detail to be gleaned from these papers, there are serious gaps in the archives. Surviving correspondence is generally one-sided: President Case kept numerous wartime letters addressed to him, but aside from the occasional draft reply, correspondence sent from Corpus remained with the intended recipients. Detailed Governing Body minutes were kept throughout the war; but other College bodies, such as the Servants' Committee, met infrequently and made only very brief notes of sessions. Corpus Library and Archives have a complete run of back issues of the *Pelican Record*, providing us with an excellent 'official' picture of the College during 1914–18; but anecdotes on more personal and everyday wartime College life, as experienced by those within its walls, do not feature.

Such caveats aside, this book explores four aspects of the College's wartime life and experiences by drawing almost exclusively on material housed within the College's Library and special collections, supplemented by texts from war historians. Firstly, we shall see how the outbreak and continuation of the war affected Corpus Governing Body and policy-making. The second chapter focuses on Corpus's wartime student casualties, exploring some individual stories of those who were killed at the front and those who survived but returned with wounds; and examines the experiences of Corpus's only known conscientious objector. Chapter 3 discusses the impact of the war on

Corpus servants, looking both at the servants who died and fought in the trenches, and those who remained at Corpus throughout the conflict. Finally, we shall look at how the war affected the College itself throughout the years 1914–18, seeing how its buildings were put to use, and discovering what everyday life was like for the individuals who studied, taught, worked or resided there during the war and its aftermath.

Harriet Patrick
April 2018

1

CORPUS'S PRESIDENT AND
FELLOWS IN WARTIME

Pre-War Corpus

Early 20th-century Corpus Christi was the smallest college in the University of Oxford, apart from the associated Permanent Private Halls. Although Corpus, in the decades preceding the First World War, showed some interest in a wider range of studies for its undergraduates, 'its principal investment lay first in Classics and then in philosophy'.[1] Given Corpus's concentration on Classics, the College depended on having 'a high reputation among those schools that produced the best classicists' and wished to maintain this high reputation in order for such schools to 'send their best candidates to compete for Corpus scholarships'.[2] This explains why editors of the *Pelican Record* in 1891 were 'glad to observe that the larger public schools are well represented amongst the men elected to scholarships and exhibitions last March'.[3] 23 freshmen had matriculated during Michaelmas Term in 1913 (17 had done so in 1912), and during that final peacetime academic year a total of 71 junior members were in residence, overseen by 15 Fellows, two Lecturers and President Thomas Case. Given Corpus's prevailing 'concentration on Classics',[4] most of these young men had arrived from England's minor public schools and the majority of them read Literae Humaniores. Still others studied Modern History; and a small number read Jurisprudence, Mathematics, Medicine, or undertook Pass Schools, studying a variety of amalgamated modules. After graduating, most Corpuscles pursued careers in the Church, the law or the civil service, or became schoolmasters.[5] Pre-war Corpus was a very small community with an overwhelmingly public-school flavour.

Records regarding pre-war College servants are patchier: it is unclear from the records exactly how many servants were employed by Corpus during the year 1913–14. However, we do know that at Michaelmas 1904 there were 25 individuals listed on the staff, not including the Bursar, Henry Le Blanc Lightfoot: one butler, helped by an under butler; a manciple ('in overall control of catering'[6]), assisted by a cook and two kitchen apprentices; a Common Room man, with two understudies; a porter, with the help of an under porter; seven bedmakers ('fore runners of today's scouts'[7]), supported by three under bedmakers; one messenger; a gardener; one bootblack; and the College clerk. There is nothing in the archives to indicate that staffing levels changed significantly over the next decade, so it seems safe to assume that this body of College servants remained at around 25 in number until the outbreak of war in 1914.

Physically, the Corpus of 1913 was very similar to how it is today: the main Quad, Cloisters and Fellows' Building were all in continual academic and residential use. Undergraduates ate dinner in Hall – but had breakfast and lunch in their rooms – and studied in the Library, though what is now the ground floor of the Library then included Lecture Room 3, accessible via a door opposite the Chapel. Chapel was almost universally attended on Sundays during full University term. What is now the Old Lodgings was, in the early 20th century, the residence of the College President, and had been the home of President Thomas Case and his family since 1904.

When not studying, early 20th-century Corpuscles had several extracurricular activities in which to participate. The period from the late 1880s up to the First World War 'was the golden age of College societies'.[8] Sports teams included the Boat Club, Rugby, Football, Hockey, Lawn Tennis and Cricket but the special novelty of this time was 'the multiplication of non-sporting College societies'.[9] The Pelican Essay Club, founded in November 1881, held weekly meetings in which an individual member's essay was read aloud, followed by a group discussion. The Owlet Club, established in 1889 following the discontinuance of its predecessor, the Minerva Club, met for weekly dramatic readings; the society, in an adapted form, still exists today. Other contemporary extracurricular groups included the Church Society and the Tenterden Essay Club, which held weekly meetings to 'read and discuss papers on subjects chiefly literary'.[10] Corpus's magazine, the *Pelican Record*, was established in 1891, and was edited from its conception until 1909 by Arthur Sidgwick (CCC Fellow 1882–1902 and 1904–20) with a succession of junior fellow-editors.[11] Also popular with Corpuscles were the Wasps Dining Club, founded in May 1900, which held meetings once a week during term time; and the Sundial Society, a debating and discussion club founded in February 1910. Corpus's low student numbers meant that many of the same young men were in multiple groups and knew each other very well. The College Boat Club, first established in 1858, kept detailed annals of its crews and races in the Captain's Book; six of its crew members for 1913–14 were also members of the Pelican Essay Club in that year, as were seven members of Corpus's Rugby XV.

Whilst the overwhelming majority of undergraduate socialising happened within College, there was one University-wide activity which became increasingly popular during the years preceding the outbreak of war: the Oxford University Officers' Training Corps (OTC). Rising militarism was palpable within both Oxford and Corpus before 1914. Editors of the December 1909 issue of the *Pelican Record* observed that membership of the College shooting team was growing.

> It is interesting to note a considerable recrudescence of military enthusiasm in the College of late. It would indeed be surprising, in view of the recent revival in Oxford, if Corpus were entirely unaffected by the military spirit. We hear reports of a high place in inter-Collegiate shooting. All success to the team. If not military ourselves, we are not anti-militant.[12]

Six months later, editors congratulated Corpus's detachment of the OTC 'on being bracketed second with Hertford in the Drill Competition for the Bourne Cup'. The College detachment was now 33 strong, in contrast to summer 1908 when 'only two members of the college belonged to the University Volunteers'; and the *Pelican*'s editors would soon consider 'devoting a special page to the doings of the O.T.C.'.[13] By December 1910 the Corpus detachment of the OTC had increased to 40,[14] although by the end of 1912 it numbered only 25.[15]

Although the University experienced a rise in militarism, 'there was no premonition in the first part of 1914 of the impending cataclysm'.[16] Indeed in June 1914 the University 'formally celebrated the profound contribution of German culture to European arts and learning'[17] when it conferred honorary degrees upon a number of German individuals. Among others, Richard Strauss received a doctorate in music and a doctorate in civil law was conferred on the German ambassador.[18] Before the outbreak of war, Oxford's links with Germany were close, with a steady stream of scholars seeking postgraduate experience at the prestigious German universities. Corpus shared this enthusiasm. The March 1914 issue of the *Pelican Record* features a lengthy article by Corpuscle Revd Canon Henry Balmforth (CCC 1909–13) entitled 'In a German University' which describes, in great detail, Balmforth's visit to the University of Göttingen and his favourable impressions of student life and learning there.[19] The First World War 'severed this Anglo-German cultural tie'.[20] When war broke out in August 1914 it seemed to take much of the University by surprise. Also unexpected was the length of the conflict and the scale of the carnage. Noticeable was the *Pelican Record*'s decidedly optimistic view expressed in December 1914: 'it is hoped that next October will find us at peace and at normal work again.'[21]

President Thomas Case

Corpus Christi's 23rd President, Thomas Case, had been elected by the College ten years before the outbreak of war, and remained in post until 1924. Born in 1844 to Robert Case, a Liverpool stockbroker, and Esther (née MacMillan), Case had been educated at Rugby School and Balliol College, where he obtained a first in Literae Humaniores in 1867. Before becoming President at Corpus, he had worked briefly at the Stock Exchange; spent a year as assistant master at Cheltenham College; and become a fellow, tutor and lecturer at Balliol College in 1870. He married Elizabeth Donn, daughter of the composer Sir William Sterndale Bennett, in 1870, and the couple had two sons and a daughter. Case was evidently a somewhat eccentric figure, and throughout his presidency he managed to antagonise many members of the College's Governing Body. In his memoirs, George Beardoe Grundy (CCC Fellow 1903–21) described Case as 'the most pronounced individualist I have ever come across': when it came to University matters, Case was a 'rigid conservative' who determinedly opposed the abolition of compulsory Greek, the admission of women, and 'what he considered the exaggerated claims of science'.[22] Whilst pre-war Oxford's academic affinity, especially in the Classics, lay towards Germany more than to any other country, Case's personal opinions may have alienated a less scholarly general public, for 'he regarded the German race as the most capable nation in the world'.[23] A further tragedy of the First World War, especially for a classical college like Corpus, was that it fractured what had been up to 1914 a major scholarly international alliance. In his speech surveying the events of the academic year 1913–14, the University of Oxford's Vice Chancellor T. B. Strong said, 'We have taken up arms against the one power in Europe with which we [and he might have added "especially Corpus, and especially Case within Corpus"] have had closest affinity.'[24] Our knowledge of Case's thoughts and opinions during the war is naturally limited: we can only interpret the papers that made their way to the Archives. Nonetheless, he did keep significant numbers of wartime papers, which can help to shed light on him as an individual of interest.

When war was declared on 4 August 1914, Thomas Case and his wife Elizabeth were away from Oxford, holidaying in Weymouth. Administrative correspondence thus flew back and forth between Case on the Dorset coast and College Bursar Henry Le Blanc Lightfoot at Corpus. The dates of the letters between the two parties testify to the speed and efficiency of the wartime postal service. On the day after the outbreak of war, Lightfoot wrote to inform Case that the administrator of the Third Southern General Hospital, Major E. C. Foster, had requested the 48 beds which Corpus had previously stated that it could supply in case of emergency, and that other colleges were receiving similar notices. His letter continued:

> New College, and I believe Keble, are full of the Oxford Territorials who have taken up their Quarters there.
>
> Plummer [CCC Fellow 1873–1927, Chaplain 1875–1927] is leaving Oxford for Salisbury today, so there will be no one resident in College. I understand that he is attending today at Head Quarters to give certification as to character to any Corpus men who are taking up Commissions. I hear from the Porter that Malcolm is coming up tonight [Pulteney Malcolm (CCC 1913–14) had been summoned to Oxford by the Nomination Board of the OTC].
>
> The Vice Chancellor is sitting at Head Quarters for 2 hours daily, presiding over a Committee of the O.O.T. Corps, to I presume sign certificates to Undergraduates who are taking up Commissions.[25]

Such a flurry of activity within just 24 hours of the war's outbreak foreshadows how greatly Oxford, effectively a military garrison town, would be affected by the conflict. It also indicates the widespread popularity of the war and the downright eagerness of young men to enlist. Case did not share this enthusiasm for war.

Upon receipt of Lightfoot's communication of 5 August, Case replied in a letter the next day that, regarding the beds, 'I do not see that anything is to be done except to hand them over'. Case mistakenly thought that the authorities wanted to take over the College kitchen, sighing, 'I suppose they will have to manage that too'. On 8 August he wrote to the Bursar of his 'great relief' to hear that Corpus was just to hand over its beds to the military hospital, lately established in the Examination Schools, and was not itself due to become a hospital. Aware that the College had the first call on him, Case stated that if Lightfoot thought he should be at Corpus, he would 'return when necessary'. However, he also wrote that his room was booked until 13 August and that he was making such good progress on his book (work which Case was never destined to finish) that he would 'rather remain as long as my health stands the strain of hard work'.[26] Case must have found himself in a very difficult position: his rigid sense of duty to Corpus seems to have been at odds with his reluctance to assist – however remotely – with preparations for a war for which he felt little enthusiasm, perhaps even disliked. Grundy noted that Case's opposition to the war while residing in Weymouth was such that 'he blocked the way for a company of recruits marching down the street, refused to move, and had to be forcibly conducted to the sidewalk'.[27]

As the days and weeks went on, Case received veritable floods of letters from numerous undergraduates asking for advice about volunteering for military service, telling of commissions received, and reporting of decisions to enlist. Case's response, according to Grundy, was to tell 'various undergraduates that if they volunteered for service they would not thenceforth be regarded as belonging to the college'.[28] This distorts Case's outlook, but he was certainly reluctant to see his undergraduates fight in the war rather than continue with their studies when term resumed in October. The first of these letters which Case received, dated 5 August, was from E. S. Carter (CCC 1911–14). Within a week this was followed by letters from nine others: E. Hale (Scholar-elect, CCC 1917–20), G. B. Ramsbotham (CCC 1912–14), N. T. Porter (CCC 1913–14), R. C. Wace (CCC 1913–14), R. W. M. Dewhurst (CCC Scholar-elect 1914), R. O. Hobhouse (CCC 1911–14), E. F. Clarke (CCC 1913–14), D. Hussey (CCC 1912–14), and W. P. Griffiths (CCC Scholar-elect 1914). Case's response to all of these letters, and the dozens of others that followed in successive weeks, was described in his *Report of the President on the Connexions of the College with the Present War*, written for Governing Body on 11 September 1914:

> On the whole, I concluded that it was my duty in the exceptional circumstances to give to those undergraduates who desired to serve in the War every facility consistent with the Statutes of the College, the continuity of its tuition, and its power of determining what was to be done with its undergraduates serving in the War during their absence and afterwards.
>
> Accordingly, in the answers which I have written to the letters

of undergraduates, I have invariably given them leave of absence; and that, too, whether they asked leave or not, and whether they had asked leave before they volunteered or after they had committed themselves. Then, I have always informed them that the Vice-Chancellor has given notice that he will propose a Decree to postpone their examinations; and that this Decree, when carried, will affect, but not govern, the decision of the College. Next, in answering a Scholar or Exhibitioner, I have referred to Statute 31 (e), and said that it would be for the College to determine in October whether it had sufficient reason to pay his emolument during non-residence, and what it would do afterwards. In no case did I attempt to usurp the place of a parent by encouragement or discouragement of a son's ambition to serve. When, however, in one or two cases my correspondent said that he depended entirely on his University career, I advised him to hesitate. Only in dealing with one class of cases, I thought it my duty to point out to under-graduates the danger of breaking their University career. Several of the undergraduates, who desired to volunteer, are candidates for Literae Humaniores next Midsummer. To them I said that, supposing they were absent for a year, and had their examina-tion postponed to Midsummer 1916, they would forget much in the year, and then would have only 9 months to recover and improve for a School, which essentially requires continuous study. But this was only advice, which they have usually not followed.

Finally, as I have in all cases given leave of absence on the conditions I have mentioned, I have given the undergraduates every facility to serve consistent with the Statutes of the College.[29]

That Case felt compelled to justify his response to the outbreak of war to his colleagues, and to describe it in such detail, reflects the somewhat turbulent relationship between Corpus's President and the rest of Governing Body. It also demonstrates Case's determination to see the College abide by its rules and regulations, and his general aversion to flexibility. His *Report* was a detailed document at 16 pages long; and Case had gone to the trouble of having it professionally printed before circulating it to Governing Body. It also testifies to how unusual was Case's ambivalence towards the war in comparison to the more fervent attitudes held by the majority in 1914.

It is clear that, relations with members of Governing Body aside, Case was highly regarded by undergraduates and their families. Throughout the war, he continued to receive letters from Corpuscles telling of their lives during training and fighting; he was also sent numerous heart-wrenching letters from the young men's families conveying news of their deaths. Several of these contained testimonies of how Corpus, and Case, had shaped the students' attitude to life and had powerfully affected their sense of honour and duty. In October 1915 Case received a letter from Revd Arthur Caynton Radcliffe (CCC 1872–5) regarding his son, William Yonge Radcliffe, who had been due to follow his father and come up to Corpus as a commoner in 1914. W. Y. Radcliffe had died of wounds received in action at Gallipoli in August, and his father wrote that 'his name must therefore be taken off the list of those intending to come into residence at C.C.C. after the war. As he was my only son, there is now no hope of my retaining a connection with the college through the next generation.'[30] Radcliffe's grief at his son's death was evidently sharpened by the break in the link to his old College. Although Radcliffe would not have known Case personally (attending Corpus as he did under President John Wilson), he nonetheless felt compelled to write this letter; and Radcliffe was by no means the only parent to write to Case of personal loss. In May 1915 Case received another moving letter from R. B. Ramsbotham, the brother of Corpus Scholar G. B. Ramsbotham, who had enlisted in 1914. Ramsbotham had been killed in action on 16 May while storming the German lines at Festubert. The letter continued:

I take the liberty of writing to tell you how dearly he loved his college, and of the affectionate respect that he had for yourself, sir, personally. I hope, when I get my leave, that I may be able to come and see his rooms in the College which he loved so well.

I think that Geoffrey, like many Corpus men, had a very high sense of duty, and that the College emblem of the Pelican plucking its breast was of very real significance to him. Well he gave his lifeblood for England, and he died like an English gentleman.

I'm so proud to think he was a scholar of C.C.C.

Forgive my trespassing on your time – but I thought you would like to know that Geoffrey was very proud to be on the foundation of your College.[31]

Case had in fact received semi-regular correspondence from G. B. Ramsbotham throughout his military service, the last of which was dated 1 March 1915, a mere ten weeks before he was killed: the news of Ramsbotham's death cannot have failed to affect Case personally. That letter was closely followed by news of the death of another Corpuscle near Festubert on 15 June 1915, James George Gee Janasz (CCC 1912–14), sent by the boy's father. 'His death is a terrible blow to us, but we were very thankful he had strength given him to do his duty for our King and country as well as for the sake of humanity.'[32] Mr Janasz also included a copy of Colonel Walter S. Brown's letter dated 18 June 1915:

His Captain, who is the only Officer not hit in the two leading Companies, could not say enough in his praise today.

England can ill afford to lose such men as these, the Regiment feels his loss; but we all know what a terrible blow it must be to you. I hardly like to take the liberty of troubling you with a letter at this sad time; but felt I must express to you our great admiration of your son, and our deepest sympathy with you in your bereavement.

In his file of wartime correspondence which now resides in the College Archives, Case kept similar letters from the families and friends of three other Corpuscles killed in service: W. J. Newton (CCC Commoner 1879),[33] J. C. Stokoe (CCC 1912–15)[34] and G. O. W. Willink (CCC 1907–11).[35] He also received letters from dozens of Corpuscles themselves throughout the war, many of whom were killed in the violence of the conflict. While Case kept these particular letters, we cannot be sure how many others, if any, he may have received. It is impossible to know the nature of what Case said in any of his own correspondence to Corpuscles at the front, though it seems unlikely that he went to the same lengths as Sir Herbert Warren, his contemporary counterpart at Magdalen College. While Case certainly received tens of letters from Corpuscles at the front, Magdalen College Archives contain over 1,000 letters that were sent to President Warren from old members or their relatives in the course of the war. Moreover, when responding to these letters Warren 'always found something to say that would convince a grieving parent that he had really known their "boy", even when the undergraduate's inclinations had not perfectly gelled with his own'. These condolence letters 'were always accompanied by an appeal for a photograph of the deceased, and details of his death. The information he invariably received was then transferred to his three grand memorial volumes of the Magdalen dead.'[36] Case's wartime correspondence with junior members is unlikely to have been deficient, but he certainly did not undertake Warren's Herculean efforts to correspond with undergraduates and their families in a war-torn world.

But of course it was not just military correspondence pertaining to undergraduates which required Case's attention. On 17 August 1914, Corpus Fellow R. B. Mowat wrote to Case with the information that a College servant, Arthur Edward Blagrove, a trained soldier, was also seeking permission to enlist. Blagrove had joined Corpus aged 21 on 15 February 1909, when he was appointed as under porter; he was subsequently appointed bedmaker in October 1913.

> But he would only go if he can get some idea of his future, that is if the College will promise to keep his place open for him. He is unmarried. I have not done anything on the subject, except to write this to you. He would be glad to hear the decision as soon as practicable, so as to get away with the trained men. I told him the question would not be settled at once. Personally I sympathise with him. He is very respectful, and made the request in a modest way.[37]

Case was horrified by the prospect. Once more, finding his feelings somewhat at odds with the rest of the Governing Body, he summarised his reaction in his *Report* of September 1914:

I communicated [Blagrove's] application to the Bursar. I said that whatever I did for him will affect the tenure of service of every servant of the College for the future, that we cannot know till October what the College would answer to his application, and that, if he volunteers, he does so at his peril ... I have had a long experience of servants, of the disastrous loss of control of servants by masters, and of the consequent decline of the efficiency of work ... I consider that to allow a servant of the College to leave his work to go on military service, with a promise of reinstatement on his return, would be a departure from the existing terms of the employment of a servant by the College, and would tend to form a precedent in favour of the tendency towards fixity of tenure. On the other hand, I am not saying that in the exceptional circumstances of the War this leave will not be given to Blagrove by the College. But what I do say is that neither I, nor the Servants' Committee, nor any authority except the College can promise to keep his place open for him; and indeed it is this promise of the College for which he asked according to Mr Mowat's letter of August 17th, and without which he finally agreed not to go.[38]

Case saw the College Statutes as sacrosanct, and business inside its walls as more important than anything that might be happening outside, even war. That his colleagues did not share his views prompted both bewilderment in Case and a hotbed of conflict between him and the rest of Governing Body. When Grundy, who had been a Fellow at Corpus since 1903 (a year before Case's appointment as President), informed Case on 27 August 1914 that he had offered his services to the War Office, Case was incandescent with rage. In his reply two days later, Case demanded that Grundy retract his offer to the Government, or else resign as Tutor to Corpus. Much of this anger was the result of his misunderstanding the nature of Grundy's offer: Case thought that Grundy had offered to assist with war work at the expense of his academic duties, rather than in addition to them. On 30 August Grundy explained in exasperation that

I am willing to give my services till the term begins; and that I would be willing to give them after that date provided that my college gave me leave to do so. That is a perfectly legitimate offer, and it is not going to be withdrawn.

I understand that every other college in the University is doing all in its power to make it possible for its tutors, undergraduates, and college servants to serve their country at this most critical time. I am very much surprised at your attitude in this matter; but I should be still more surprised if the Governing Body of the college adopted it.[39]

Case was greatly relieved to hear of his misunderstanding, but the damage had already been done. The College made moves to bypass, if necessary, what they saw as the President's reluctance to assist in the war effort by holding a private meeting on 3 September. Here the nine other members of Governing Body unanimously agreed that 'every facility' should be given to 'Fellows, Officers of the College, Undergraduates and Servants of the College to undertake service at the present time in connexion with the War', and that, in order that this opinion may be discussed, 'a meeting of Residents be called with the least possible delay'.[40]

Against this backdrop of rebellion, Case had little choice but to admit defeat. He managed to avoid the 'meeting of Residents' requested, but complied with their other demand during the Governing Body meeting of 10 October. Case's *Report* had served to explain, and to some extent apologise for, his original stance to his colleagues:

I have written this Report, not to blame anybody, but to defend myself against the suspicion of having been backward in giving facilities for service in the War, whereas in reality I was doing all I could consistently with the Statutes of the College. There will be a General Meeting of the College on Saturday, October 10th, when I hope and trust that all our differences will give way to the good of the College. In the words of one of the Fellows, who has written me a letter on this subject, 'it is vitally important that we should stand together and co-operate to help the College through the evil times in store for it.'[41]

Case was thus defeated on his initial stance, but his misgivings about the war certainly remained, in particular his fears about what might occur if its democratic potential was followed through. Writing in *The Times* in June 1917 he warned that

> this nation is in danger of drifting into revolution unprepared, like France in 1789; but it will be a revolution far more dangerous, because it has been organised beforehand by persons accustomed to the use of might against right, and ready at any moment for the overthrow of the existing fabric of society by the combined agency of the State and trade unionism.[42]

Fellows on Active Service and Other Wartime Work

Thus it was not just undergraduates of Corpus who were keen to be involved in the war effort: a number of College Fellows also volunteered for national service; or, failing that, offered to help in other ways that played to their strengths. In the end, only three academics from Corpus saw military action at the front. The first of these was William Phelps (CCC Fellow 1906–50). Born in Dulwich in 1882, he was a scholar at Balliol College, obtained a first in Literae Humaniores in 1905 and became a Fellow at Corpus in the following year, aged just 24. Not yet 32 when the war broke out in August 1914, Phelps was young enough for active service. He duly volunteered, and his progress was reported in the *Pelican Record*. By December the magazine's editors noted,

> We have pleasure in congratulating Mr Phelps on his appointment as lieutenant to the 7th (Service) Battalion Oxford and Bucks Light Infantry. He was first of all stationed on Salisbury Plain, where conditions were none of the best. Now, very luckily, he is billeted in his rooms in College, but owing to his arduous military duties very little is seen of him during the day.[43]

By March 1916 Phelps had left for France; nine months later, the magazine declared,

It is with pleasure that we record the promotion to the rank of Major of Captain W. Phelps of the Lancashire Fusiliers. It will be remembered that Mr Phelps received a commission in the 7th Service Batt. of the Oxford and Bucks L.I. soon after the outbreak of war, but was subsequently transferred to his present regiment. All his contemporaries at Corpus will join in congratulating him on obtaining his majority.[44]

Phelps served in France until 1919. He then returned to Corpus where, as June's *Pelican* editors noted, 'Mr Phelps has exchanged the trench for the cloister.'[45] He continued as a Fellow at Corpus until 1950, dying in 1963.

Meanwhile, William McDougall (CCC Fellow 1912–20) also saw the impact of war at first hand. Born in Lancashire in 1871, he had been educated privately; but he had also studied at the Real-Gymnasium in Weimar before becoming a student in Manchester and going on to study Natural Sciences at Cambridge. Thereafter he was a medical student at St Thomas's Hospital, London, and went on to work as an academic in Cambridge, London and Oxford. In 1912 he was elected a Fellow of the Royal Society. At Oxford he was Wilde Reader in Mental Philosophy. He had been at Corpus for only two years before war was declared. At the outbreak of war McDougall, like many others, favoured assisting Oxford's war effort however possible: he 'supported the decision to provide temporary accommodation for recruits in the college in September 1914'.[46] During the conflict, he served as a major in the Royal Army Medical Corps (RAMC) from 1915 to 1919. But McDougall was not just interested in the care of physical wounds; as a psychologist he was also concerned in caring for soldiers' psychological damage. Shell shock was gradually recognised as a medical condition during the war; and by 1917 he was treating patients with many different symptoms at the Base Hospital.[47] After peace was declared, McDougall remained at Corpus until 1920, serving as the College's Vice President, in which capacity he continued to assist the College in the war's after-effects. Acting as President for Michaelmas 1918, McDougall put much of his house 'at the disposal of the College for the benefit of scholarship candidates who this year would have found it so difficult to find accommodation in Oxford that the necessity of postponing the examinations until after Term had very seriously to be considered'.[48] Thereafter he was appointed professor of psychology at Harvard University, 1920–7. He remained in the US until his death on 28 November 1938.

The final Corpus academic to see active service was Bertram Lambert, born in 1881 (CCC Lecturer in Chemistry 1909–21). During the conflict Lambert served as a major in the Royal Engineers; he also served as staff major and chemical adviser to the Inspector General of Communications in the British Expeditionary Force. Thus the few scientists who remained at Corpus during the war had to receive tuition elsewhere in the University: 'In the absence of Mr Lambert, those undergraduates of the College who are reading science will be under the charge of Mr F. D. Chattaway and Dr Vernon [Horace Middleton Vernon (1870–1951), physiologist and industrial health specialist, appointed fellow of Magdalen in 1898, and Oxford University lecturer in chemical physiology 1915–19].'[49] After the Armistice, Lambert returned and continued his lectureship at Corpus until 1921, when he became a fellow and tutor in Chemistry at Merton College, and Oxford's Aldrichian Praelector in Chemistry, 1920–47. He died on 1 July 1963.

Other Fellows of Corpus offered themselves to the war effort away from the front. Perhaps the most intriguing of this war work was undertaken by G. B. Grundy. Born in Wallasey, Cheshire, in 1861, Grundy was educated at Risley School and Lichfield Grammar School before becoming an undergraduate at Brasenose 1888–91, where he obtained a second in Literae Humaniores. He went on to gain his MA in 1894 and DLitt in 1902; he was also awarded Oxford's Arnold History Essay Prize in 1899 and the Conington Prize in 1900. In 1891 he married Mabel, daughter of Dr George Rice Ord; the couple had a son and a daughter. During the 1890s Grundy had worked as a tutor in Oxford, but also spent time surveying in Greece, Syracuse, Romania and Transylvania. It was this work which proved useful to the War Office when he volunteered his services in August 1914. At the outbreak of war Grundy initially volunteered for active service; but, at 53, his offer was rejected on grounds of age. Instead, in October 1914 he was 'summoned to London by telegram to do work for the War Office, namely, a route-book for northern Greece and Macedonia'. Captain Reginald Hall, director of Naval Intelligence at the Admiralty, proposed that Grundy should draw up a memorandum on the coasts of Greece, since 'there were details that the Admiralty charts did not include with regard to the small bays and inlets where U-boats might lurk'. As an esteemed classicist with an intimate knowledge of the area, Grundy was an obvious choice for this somewhat unusual intelligence work. He duly spent a year working on his route-book. When it was finished, Grundy was asked to prepare a similar book on Rumelia. This, however, he declined, citing lack of familiarity; instead he 'recommended that the work should be done by a friend of mine who knew far more of Rumelia than I did'.[50]

Grundy continued with his academic responsibilities alongside his work for the War Office. But as the years wore on, the war still continued to rage and the College saw its number of members in residence drop further. Thus he found that more military demands were made upon his time, and he became a temporary civil servant for the Admiralty in 1916. The *Pelican Record* noted that, 'as the numbers of the flock fall, those of the shepherds equally decrease. Dr Grundy and Mr Mowat have transferred their energies for a part of the week from the study of past, to the making of present, history, and are employed in work at the Admiralty.'[51] Once he had finished working for the Admiralty, Grundy became a timber valuer for the government, valuing timber in Oxfordshire, Buckinghamshire, Northamptonshire and Hertfordshire for military use. Grundy later wrote of this work, 'in two years I dealt with more than a hundred owners of timber. With but two exceptions they were most patriotic in their attitude towards the Government demands, though they would obviously have liked to keep their woodland.'[52] Grundy thus found himself in varied and colourful war work over the years.

Grundy was not the only member of his family actively involved in the war effort. His wife Mabel, a rather remarkable woman, found herself called upon to assist with the war effort in a different, though perhaps no less unusual, capacity than her husband. In September 1914 thousands of men across the country offered themselves as recruits, and came much faster than they could be enrolled. Problems in Oxford became serious when 'several hundreds of men gathered there waiting for enrolment, a large number of whom were without the means of paying for board and lodging'. The town mayor called on Mabel Grundy and

> asked her whether she and some friends of hers could provide a supper every day at the town hall for some hundreds of men, the first of which should take place within twenty-four hours. To get food for hundreds of people and the cooks to cook it within twenty-four hours was a tall proposition; but they did it.

She carried on for some time. Later, Mrs Grundy was asked to help with catering for 'a large Army hospital in Oxford holding several hundred patients', which she did for two years. Afterwards, she 'was asked to organise food control in Oxford'. Subsequently Mabel Grundy was elected to the Town Council and made a JP in the first list of women magistrates ever issued.[53] In 1915 Dr and Mrs Grundy's daughter, Barbara May, became engaged to Corpuscle Hugh Faithful Chittenden (CCC 1911–14). The couple were married on 9 April 1917 at St Peter-in-the-East, Oxford, by Revd H. W. Boustead, assisted by Canon Skrine and Revd E. C. Summers. During the war Chittenden served in the Royal Sussex Regiment and the Royal Engineers, seeing service in France and Belgium. He was awarded the Military Cross in 1917, was mentioned in despatches in 1918, and survived the conflict. Mr and Mrs Chittenden went on to have two sons, the eldest of whom, Hugh John Robert Chittenden, also came to Corpus in 1937. H. J. R. Chittenden left Oxford two years later without sitting any University exams in order to serve in the Second World War. He was killed in active service in Mombasa on 30 October 1942 aged 24.[54]

Other Fellows found war work as civil servants, including Arthur Ernest Jolliffe (CCC Fellow 1891–1920). Born in Oxford in 1871, he was educated at Oxford High School and Balliol College, where he obtained a first in Mathematics in 1891, and was just 20 when appointed Fellow of Corpus. Jolliffe worked as a temporary civil servant in the Ministry of Munitions in 1915–16. Editors of the College magazine for December 1915 wrote to congratulate him on his 'useful and honourable' position held in public service, but hoped that the College would see him back again soon.[55] Robert Balmain Mowat (CCC Fellow 1907–28) served in a similar way. Born in Edinburgh in 1883, he attended the University of Edinburgh and Balliol College, obtaining a first in Literae Humaniores in 1905. During the war Mowat served as a temporary civil servant, working for the Naval Intelligence Department, War Cabinet Secretariat, and as an aide to General Smuts at Versailles. At the beginning of 1919 Mowat was 'suddenly summoned by the Government to Paris in connexion with the Peace Conference', and Austin Lane Poole, Fellow of St John's College, was appointed to act as Modern History Tutor in Mowat's absence at a rate of £5 a term per man, paid for by Mowat.[56] Poole's appointment was terminated by Mowat's return to Corpus in the spring. Thereafter, Mowat continued to work as a Fellow until 1928, when he was appointed as a professor of history at Bristol University, a post he held until his death in an air accident on 2 September 1941.[57] Similarly, Sir Richard Winn Livingstone (CCC Fellow 1904–24), whose tenure as Fellow and Assistant Tutor at Corpus exactly matched Case's appointment as President, undertook civil service work. Livingstone was born in Liverpool in 1880 and became a scholar at New College 1899–1903. In 1915 he was employed by the Ministry of Munitions, where he continued working until 1916. The *Pelican Record* happily recorded the birth of Livingstone's eldest son, Richard Percy, during this time:

> We have the pleasure of congratulating Mr and Mrs Livingstone on the birth of a son. It is events like this that relieve the gloom of a European War, and give promise of continued strength for England in the future. We are sure that Master Livingstone will justify all the hopes that are entertained of him, and we trust that he will become, like his father, a distinguished member of Corpus.[58]

The boy did indeed go on to study at Corpus later, from 1933 to 1936. R. P. Livingstone later served during the Second World War: he was mentioned in despatches, and was awarded an MBE in 1943.

Elsewhere, Fellows found their teaching 'outsourced' from Corpus

as part of war work. Like Grundy before them, Jolliffe and Livingstone must have found demands on their time as academic Tutors and
Fellows at Corpus wane significantly following students' enlistment
and eventual compulsory conscription in 1916. Unlike the universities,
Britain's schools continued to function fully as educational institutions because their pupils were too young to fight, but headmasters
struggled to retain teachers, resorting to hiring female staff and
retired masters to teach the boys. Presumably it was in this capacity of
needing qualified teaching staff that Jolliffe was appointed as acting
assistant master at Radley College, Berkshire in 1916, employment
that qualified as war work. This appointment evidently only lasted for
a year. At the end of 1917 Radley College's magazine, *The Radleian*,
noted that 'We accord a hearty welcome to Mr. Kirkby, the late Sub-
Warden, who has returned temporarily, after three years absence,
to take the place of Mr. Jolliffe, whose services are required by the
Government.'[59] Afterwards Jolliffe returned to Corpus; thereafter he
left upon being appointed professor of mathematics at the University
of London's Royal Holloway College in 1920. Similarly, Livingstone
found himself filling in for absent schoolteachers during the conflict;
he was appointed assistant master at Eton College in 1917–18. Livingstone then returned to Corpus in 1919. Three years later, he was sent
a copy of the *Biography and Account of the Death of George Willink*,
a moving testimony of G. O. W. Willink, who was killed in action
on 28 March 1918. Willink's father, co-author of the biography with
his surviving son, sent the work to Livingstone along with a letter
describing the book. 'As time goes on I do not miss him less, and I
long to do anything to preserve a record of his personality.' Mr Willink
left some blank pages in the book in case Livingstone or anybody else
at Corpus wished to add anything, either cuttings from the *Pelican*
or including their own memories of the boy. His letter concluded,
'You will appreciate the colours of the "end papers" – Eton blue
at the beginning, and a fiery red at the end – this red with the dark
blue leather hinting also at C.C.C. and Alma Mater.'[60] Willink had
studied Modern History at Corpus, so would probably not have been
tutored by Livingstone personally; nevertheless it was Livingstone who
received a copy of the biography for Corpus, rather than the President

or a Modern History Fellow. Perhaps Willink's father had heard of Livingstone's temporary appointment at Eton during the war, and seized the opportunity to send the work to a Fellow who, like his son, had ties to both Corpus and Eton. The biography now resides in the College Archives. Eleven years later Livingstone became Corpus's 25th President, 1933–50, thus overseeing the College during the turbulence of the Second World War.

Fellows Residing in Corpus

Although Corpus, like the rest of Oxford, was almost emptied of its student population during the war, several Fellows always remained alongside the President within its walls. Most Corpus Fellows were too old for active service; and while several were able to serve in other ways, there were those who assisted the war effort by enabling domestic institutions to continue as normal – or as normally as was possible – throughout the conflict. Stalwart Corpus Fellows Clark, Plummer, Schiller, Stewart and Vinogradoff were among those who served in this way.

The General Meeting of Saturday 10 October 1914 – the date which would, in ordinary circumstances, have been the day before undergraduates were required to be in residence for the start of term – illustrates the war's impact on the College from the beginning, and the part which its Fellows played in keeping it running. As desired, leave was granted to Grundy and Phelps; but other Fellows were keen to voice their (and, by extension, Corpus's) support for the war effort. In minute III.7 of the meeting a letter from Ferdinand Canning Scott Schiller (CCC Fellow 1897–1937) was read aloud, in which Schiller offered £200 of his stipend for the benefit of the Tuition Fund. The College 'unanimously resolved that it desires to express its grateful sense of this very generous offer; and that, should the necessity arise, the College will gladly avail itself of this offer, but trusts it may not be necessary to do so, at any rate to the full extent'.[61] Born in Othmarschen in Altona, Holstein, Germany, in 1864, Schiller had been in England since the age of 14 and had been educated at Rugby School and Balliol College before being appointed a Fellow of Corpus in 1897. His generous financial offer to the College reflected general concerns about how the conflict, denuding Corpus of its undergraduates, staff and resources, would affect its ability to function while the war raged on; although of course in August 1914 most assumed that the war would be over in a matter of months and did not dream that it would continue to rage until November 1918. This is probably why Schiller's initial offer was not taken up by the Governing Body. At a College Meeting of 12 June 1915 Schiller once again offered financial assistance, offering to contribute £100 to the Tuition Fund. This time, however, the Governing Body decided to accept: 'the College fully appreciates the notices of Dr Schiller as expressed in his letter of May 26 to the President, and accepts with gratitude the generous offer contained in it.' Further financial offers from Dr Schiller were made, and accepted, during the war. The College Meeting of 13 November 1915 accepted his offer of £200 of his stipend to the Tuition Fund for the academic year 1915–16. Then, at the College Meeting of 29 April 1916, following the proposal of a Trust by Dr Schiller at the previous meeting in February, the College approved the terms, and appointed Plummer, Jolliffe, Stewart and Clark as Trustees for five years. The object of the Trust was to ensure Corpus Tutors and Assistant Tutors 'the maximum suitable salaries' at times when the amount of Tuition Fund was insufficient.[62] Following the Armistice, the report of the Tutorial Salaries Fund at a College Meeting on 30 November 1918 recorded that they had 'accepted a further endowment of $500 Brazilian Traction Common shares from Dr Schiller'. The report was approved by the Governing Body.[63]

But it was not just the financial contributions that Schiller gave to Corpus during the war which allowed the College to function as an educational institution. Schiller, alongside other Fellows who remained, continued to teach the few Corpuscles still resident, as well as examining those coming up for scholarships. The *Pelican Record* lists the lectures given by resident Fellows throughout the four years of the conflict, as well as publications of academic texts. Schiller also taught at other colleges to help deliver university education on behalf of absent colleagues; at a meeting of 10 November 1917 the College gave retrospective assent for Schiller's 'having given three lectures at Manchester College'.[64] Following the restoration of peace in 1918, Schiller was granted leave by the College on 30 November 1918 in order 'to supervise an Advanced Student for the Ph.D.'.[65] Meanwhile Albert Curtis Clark (CCC Fellow and Corpus Professor of Latin 1913–34) filled in for the absent Livingstone in the middle years of the war. Clark was born in Salisbury in 1859 and studied at Balliol College, from where he obtained a first in Literae Humaniores in 1881. He taught at Queen's College before arriving at Corpus. As the minutes of the College Meeting of 16 October 1915 noted, 'the College desires to express its grateful thanks to Professor Clark for his kindness in undertaking Mr Livingstone's work during his absence',[66] while the *Pelican* wrote that Clark 'has generously taken the work of classical tuition upon himself'.[67] Clark's offer to stand in for the absent Livingstone was repeated in 1916. Then at a Special College Meeting of 15 June 1918, Clark was appointed to the board of Electors for the Chair of Comparative Philosophy, and Revd Charles Plummer was appointed likewise for the Chair of Romance Languages. (Plummer had been born in Sussex in 1851 and had gone to school in Tenbury and Oxford before coming to Corpus as a scholar in 1869, obtaining a first in Literae Humaniores in 1873, whereupon he became a Life Fellow of his alma mater, also acting as College Chaplain from 1875.) In November 1918, John Alexander Stewart (CCC Fellow 1909–28) was appointed to the board of Electors for the Corpus Professorship of Jurisprudence; he was also appointed as a member of the College.[68] (Born in 1846, Stewart had been Oxford University White's Professor of Moral Philosophy since 1897.)

Beyond their academic responsibilities, remaining Fellows helped to run Corpus in other ways. Fellows continued to act on various College committees (Estates, Library, Visitation of Buildings, and Inspection of the Plate). While their positions on the committees continued to rotate as before 1914, the number of Fellows under-taking war service meant that College administration matters had to be shared between the smaller number of remaining men. Fellows also found other practical ways to keep the College alive through the war. At the College Meeting held on 10 October 1914, the minutes record that 'the College gratefully accepted Mr Plummer's offer to play the organ, and Mr Sherwood's offer [Revd William Edward Sherwood

(CCC Assistant Chaplain, 30 Nov. 1912; mayor of Oxford in 1913)]
to take all the evening services during this term'. Plummer's proposal
was again offered and accepted at the meeting of 21 November 1914.
At the same meeting, following the Report of the Inspection of the
College Plate, the minutes note that 'it was resolved that the President
and Professor Clark have power to deal with the repair of the Altar
Candlesticks'. Then in May 1915 Plummer was granted leave by the
College 'to reproduce a photograph of the Satchel of the Irish Missal
in the College Library'; he was also re-elected as a governor of Chel-
tenham Grammar School for three years. During the meeting of 13
November 1915 'it was resolved that a Committee be appointed to
report on the question of installing electric lights in the Old Library
and the Study Library'. Livingstone (evidently temporarily back at
Corpus) and Clark were chosen as members of the said committee.[69]
Then in October 1916 Clark was elected as the College's Deputy
Librarian, 'to hold office during Mr Livingstone's absence'. At the
General College Meeting of the following November Clark, still acting
as Deputy Librarian, 'called attention to the question of preventing
damp in the Lower Library', whereby it was agreed to make a report
at the next meeting.[70] Meanwhile, Professor Stewart quietly assisted
his colleagues at Corpus throughout the war as a member of Library,
Plate and Estates Committees. He was also, during a College Meeting
in June 1918, elected as Vice President of Corpus for the academic year
1918–19.[71]

Meanwhile, the knighthood of residing Fellow Paul Vinogradoff
(CCC Fellow and Professor of Jurisprudence, 1904–25) was announced
in the March 1917 issue of the *Pelican Record*, where he was cordially
congratulated 'on adding this political to his many academic distinc-
tions'. The editors noted with pride that Corpus Governing Body 'has
once more a titled member', something 'not enjoyed since the death
of Lord Lochee. He, however, owed his peerage entirely to his political
career, whereas Sir Paul Vinogradoff's honour can hardly have been
wholly due to his services in sustaining our Entente with Russia, great
as we may suspect them to have been.'[72] Vinogradoff had been born at
Kostroma, Russia, in 1854. He became professor of history at Moscow
University in 1887, a position from which he resigned in 1901 because

of disagreement with his country's government; he renounced his Russian nationality in 1918. Vinogradoff's knighthood in 1917 made for more cheerful news in the College magazine amidst a torrent of reports of loss and suffering of those at the front. Earlier, in November 1915, he and his wife Louise had collected funds for Russian prisoners of war,[73] exemplifying how remaining Fellows were able to help the war effort without leaving the city. Vinogradoff remained at the College throughout the war.

Lastly, remaining Fellows enabled Corpus to continue to function as a landowner. On 17 February 1917 at a meeting of Governing Body, 'the President, the Vice-President and Prof Clark were appointed a Committee to consider the possible vacancy in the living of Longford Magna, and the Rector's letters of the parishioners' memorial were referred to the Committee.' At the same meeting, 'Mr Plummer, and failing him the Rev G. H. Bowne, was nominated a commissioner under the Incumbents Resignation Act to enquire into the desirability of the resignation of the Rev O. M. Holden and the pension [to] be allotted to him'. In the following June the President, Vice President and Plummer 'were appointed to a Committee to consider the vacancy of Byfield, and to report'. At a meeting after the Armistice Plummer was 'unanimously reappointed Governor of Cheltenham Grammar School'. At the same meeting, following the death of Revd Mr Barnes, rector of the College living of Helmdon, the President, Vice President and Plummer 'were appointed a Committee to consider the vacancy, and report to the College'.[74] It is apparent that, thanks to the willingness of the Fellows to pitch in, Corpus throughout the war managed to carry out its many roles and responsibilities outside Oxford as well as within.

2

CORPUS AT THE FRONT

Corpuscles Who Died on Active Service

Corpuscles had an extraordinarily high casualty rate during the onslaught of the First World War. Nationally, the proportion of those killed during service was about 12 per cent, while in Oxford this proportion was roughly 20 per cent. Casualty rates for individual colleges within the University varied widely; but it is accepted that, at 25.43 per cent, Corpus Christi College had the highest fatality rate of any college.[1] This percentage has been calculated from the *Oxford University Roll of Service* (1920), which records 89 Corpus casualties out of 350 who fought. However, the roll contains numerous errors and omissions. It would appear that Corpus students' actual fatality rate was 23.82 per cent, that is 91 deaths out of 382 on active service.[2] The degree of error within the *Roll of Service* for other colleges is unknown; but even at the revised rate of 23.8 per cent, Corpus's losses are still higher than those traditionally calculated for all other Oxford colleges and private halls. The reasons for Oxford's, and more specifically Corpus's, disproportionate losses in the conflict have been explored by historians. They highlight Oxford's large numbers of early enlistments, and high levels of public-school intake and commissioned officers (death rates among officers substantially exceeded those among men in the lower ranks). Simultaneously, Oxford had contrasting low levels of students reading natural sciences and other occupations exempted from military service.[3] These variations in survival rate 'were slight and probably of no great significance in determining the burden of mourning which touched every corner of the University, as it did every home in Britain'.[4]

The College's Roll of Honour provides detailed portraits of the 91 Corpuscles who died on active service.[5] The following is a selection of those students who were killed at the front; and a complete list of those killed is provided in the Appendix. Meanwhile, two Corpuscles were inadvertently omitted from the war memorial: it seems only right that their stories should be shared here.

William Percival Griffiths (CCC Scholar-elect 1914) was born on 3 May 1895 to Mrs A. Griffiths and the late Revd J. Griffiths. He became a pupil at The King's School, Worcester in 1909, after winning a King's Scholarship from Oswestry Grammar School. Thereafter his family moved to Bedford, and he attended Bedford School for the sixth form, where he was awarded a day boy scholarship in 1912. He became a school monitor and chairman of the school's debating society. During his final year at school, Griffiths was elected to an open classical scholarship of £80 a year at Corpus. He was due to come to Oxford in October 1914 but the outbreak of war destroyed his plans, and he accordingly sought President Case's advice. 'Could you give me leave to serve as a Territorial Officer during the war, if it should continue up till next term, as seems probable, and at the same time allow me to retain the Scholarship to which I was elected last December?'[6] Griffiths is omitted from both Corpus's Roll of Honour and its *Biographical Register*; and although he is mentioned in the *Oxford University Roll of Service* as having served, his death is not recorded therein. Presumably news of his death never reached Corpus; and, after his initial contact with Case in 1914, the College evidently lost track of him during the conflict. Fortunately, fuller records of him survive from his schooldays, and from these we know his fate at the front. Following the outbreak of war in August 1914 Griffiths obtained a commission in the 10th Battalion Royal Welch Fusiliers, was soon promoted to lieutenant, and was subsequently promoted captain in January 1916. He was killed in action on 30 March 1916, aged 20. He has no known grave and is commemorated on the Memorial to the Missing at Menin

Gate. Griffiths' obituary in *The Vigornian*, the magazine for The King's School, includes the following tribute from his brother:

> He was killed in reconnaisance work between the lines. Light came on before he could get back and he and his orderly were hit in the legs. They started crawling back, and when nearly up to our parapet my brother was shot through the head, death being instantaneous. He has been recommended for the Military Cross for his patrol work and for bringing in wounded men in broad daylight. He had been previously wounded. He was buried, as was fitting, between the lines.[7]

Further information is known of him at Bedford School. A telegram was sent by the War Office to Griffiths' mother on 1 April 1916 stating that he had been wounded. A second telegram on 4 April announced that he had been killed in action at Saint-Éloi. Meanwhile, Griffiths appears to have had a fiancée, a Miss Lexy Creig of 46 Sloan Street, Kemp Town, Brighton. Miss Creig wrote to the War Office requesting confirmation of Griffiths' death as she had seen a report in the *Daily Telegraph* of his being wounded, but had learnt in a 'roundabout' way from one of his relatives that he had actually been killed. It seems that the couple's engagement was either not known or not acknowledged by Mrs Griffiths.[8]

John Henry Raynard Salter (CCC Commoner-elect 1917) was presumably omitted from the College war memorial for similar reasons. Never having come up to Corpus as planned because of war service, it must have been difficult for the College to keep track of his plight. Salter is also missing from the *Oxford University Roll of Service*, though he is recorded in the College's *Biographical Register*. Salter was born on 17 December 1898, the son of Charles Edward and Annie Gertrude Salter, of Moseley House, Westbourne Grove, Scarborough. He was educated at Wellington College, Berkshire, attending the school as a boarder in Hill House from Lent Term 1913 until the end of 1916. Salter served as head of house during his last term, and played as forward for the school's Rugby XV.[9] After leaving school, he became a 2nd lieutenant in the Royal Flying Corps, and was initially reported as missing, later killed in action, on 13 October 1917. He was 18 years old.

Three other fallen Corpuscles are discussed in detail here, because a wealth of printed and archival sources reveals much of their experiences before and during their time at the front: H. L. Rayner, D. W. A. Hankey and R. W. Dugdale.

Harold Leslie Rayner (CCC 1909–13) was born in Hampstead on 18 January 1890, the second son of Edward and Mrs L. Rayner. He spent six years at Heddon Court Preparatory School before being educated at Tonbridge School, Kent, in 1904–9, where he was a member of the Rugby XV, Rowing IV and eventually captain of the school. Rayner came to Corpus with a scholarship, achieving a first in Classics Moderations in 1911 and a second in Greats two years later. Rayner's father died while Rayner was at Corpus: in both the Boat Club VIII and Pelican Essay Club photographs of 1912, Rayner can be seen wearing a black armband. Despite this personal loss, Rayner remained an active member of the Corpus community, serving as College Captain, Secretary and later Captain of the Boat Club, and Secretary and then President of the Pelican Essay Club. At a meeting of the Pelican Essay Club in January 1911, 'Mr Rayner read a paper – remarkable for its length as well as for the erudition shown therein – on the "Cycle of Cathay".'[10] After Corpus, he remained in Oxford for a further year to study for a Diploma in Geography, 1913–14. He then embarked on a voyage around the world with his mother and cousin, and it was during this trip that war was declared. Rayner came home and was commissioned in the 9th Devonshire Regiment, serving alongside his friend and fellow Corpuscle John Dalgairns Upcott (CCC 1909–12), who survived the conflict. After six months' training, Rayner left for France in July 1915, and was killed in action on the opening day of the Battle of the Somme, 1 July 1916. Throughout his year in the battlefields, Rayner regularly wrote home to his mother in England and to his brother, Edward, serving as a surgeon in the Royal Navy. A selection of these letters was subsequently printed for private circulation, and they offer valuable insight into his life and death in the trenches.[11]

Upon arriving in France on 27 July 1915 Rayner sent the following letter to his mother:

> The last sight of England – an historic part of it too – was most interesting. Darkness came on as we left the coast and we were taken in convoy by some destroyers ... We found good weather here and marched off through the harbour town in great spirits with band playing and considerable attention being paid us by the inhabitants, among whom we noted a dearth of men, women and children especially predominating. We marched to our rest camp, which is on high ground near the port and commands a splendid view like the South Devon coast. A good deal of shipping lies off the harbour mouth as though there was no war about. It is a perfect day, it is just afternoon, a brilliant blue sky with cauliflower clouds round the horizon and a good breeze, such a day we enjoyed twelve months ago between the 'Line' and Fremantle. We are under canvas here, and John [Upcott] and I share a bell tent. For lunch and dinner yesterday we went to a French restaurant, where we ate heartily and made ludicrous first attempts at talking French. It seems hard to realise that we are really in France, that it is the real active service; for one thing everything in or near the camp is English or Anglicanised and one might be almost anywhere in England instead of 'somewhere' in France ... There is much to recall our holidays in France; it seems very familiar to be here and yet it seems strange too. Just as Ed [his brother Edward] found his Gallipoli experience picnic-like we so far find it holiday-like, and the men ... are very pleased with life.[12]

The initial difficulty in believing that they were really at war shines through Rayner's description of idyllic surroundings and friendly company. This quickly changed once the men reached the front, as Rayner reflected in a letter sent to his brother on 9 August 1915:

> I got a very welcome letter from you to-day, the first I have had in the field, but far from the last I hope. It was written July 18th and refers to my midsummer letter, and in so doing seems like a voice

from another world. Those days in Bordon seem as remote from France as the pre-war days did from the time of training. Now we live a day at a time, and a year in twenty-four hours ...[13]

Censorship prevented men from describing military life in great detail to those at home; but it seems likely that few would have written harrowing accounts of life under fire even if they could have found the words to describe it, or the inclination to do so. For the most part, life consisted of long stretches of boredom intermingled with brief spikes of unutterable terror. Rayner gave his mother only vague sketches of action at the front, and was at pains to reassure her of his relative safety, as in his letter of 29 August 1915:

> Life in the fire trench, i.e., the first line, is one of very tiring and exacting routine, broken rest, snatches of sleep or none at all, wearisome standing about, and threading one's way through confusing narrow trenches, a desire for more air and elbow room never quite leaves one, although one does get used to the quite unique existence in the trenches. I have now experienced fire, support, and reserve trenches, and I expect shortly to be in billets again. I have had some more fairly narrow shaves, but I feel absolutely no fear of shells or bullets. I am glad to find it is so ...[14]

Meanwhile, Rayner's attitude towards his servant at the front, a man simply referred to as 'Wareham' in his letters, seems to have been one of paternalism: those of higher military and social status saw themselves as responsible for the safety and happiness of their men. This is reflected in a letter to his mother on 18 August 1915:

> I liked what you said about my soldier servant, he is a nice fellow, and about a week ago I slipped a note into his letter home telling his mother that I liked him and would look after him. We get on pleasantly together, and I show him quite a due amount of kindness I think. Being Devon and undemonstrative he doesn't say much in return, but I hope he appreciates it. Probably this being his first experience of such life he doesn't know if and when he is

well off. John has a nice bright fellow too, who was in the Sussex
Territorials, and not being shy, as I think Wareham is, one knows
better where one is with him, but I am quite content with my lad,
and he in his way is quite content too, I think ...[15]

Like others who fought, Rayner had few delusions about how
dangerous the conflict was at the front. On 5 September he wrote the
following letter to his brother in the lead-up to the Battle of Loos. No
similar letter to his mother appears at this time. Perhaps Rayner felt
that he could convey such thoughts to his brother who was in action
elsewhere, but not to his mother in England:

The first fortnight of September is already the chief Rayner
commemoration of the year, the 5th dear Father's death, the 10th
your birth and also Uncle William's death, and it is not impossible that 1915 is to add another date to these. I speak not out of
pessimism but out of Providence, because though it is a secret now,
it will be public property by the time you get this, that a heavy
stunt is on the programme, and we shall be in it. Writing to the
occasion is a difficult task at the best of times, and now impossible,
but this I may say in case I do not write again, it is good to have
been playing the man in these great days, and it will be to one's
credit and satisfaction that one has done so, whether one goes west
only as far as to England or to the Ultimate West. It has put the
crown to one's career up to date of eighteen months ago, and this
adventure while scattering the family to the winds, has united it
with bonds that perhaps nothing else could have forged; that too,
is so much permanent gain, so if I get scuppered in the biggest
fight in British history, there will be these thoughts to succour any
who mourn. I must stop now, but I shall try to write again while
opportunity serves.[16]

Rayner survived this particular battle with two hits to his arm, but he
fully recognised that his fate was uncertain and that next time could
be different. Writing to his mother after his experiences of the battle,
Rayner described his compulsion to put up a memorial to his fallen

comrades (three or four from his platoon that he knew of), and his own battle-weary feelings:

> Well, one fight is all I want, the sights are terrible, though fear was unknown to me; only horror possessed one when the excitement was over. One's nerves were rather strained, when after five days in the trenches we were relieved. I was so 'dog sleepy' on the march back to billets (I barely had five hours' good sleep in five days) that I saw nothing but mirages and hallucinations. The landscape changed under my eyes like a cinema film, and I saw what was not there.[17]

Fellow Corpuscle John Upcott was injured during a gas attack in the early days of the battle. Rayner wrote of this news to his mother on 8 October, 'Good old John! He got just the right sort of wound to send him home, an event everyone envies sooner or later.' The next day Rayner wrote in detail to Upcott, describing his memories of the battle which his friend missed; he subsequently wrote to Mrs Upcott to reassure her of his own survival. To his mother, he also wrote poignantly of his hopes of upcoming leave: 'at the end of this month leave will be due, and I look forward to getting it. I know it will be hard to part again after it, but the vital thing is to break the tension which we must both feel in our different spheres.'[18]

At Christmas Rayner was, as he wrote in a letter to his brother on 23 December, 'laid by the heel, thanks to an opportune attack of double febro-pharyngitis', and so celebrated the holiday in hospital in Brighton, visited by his mother. On Boxing Day he described how they had 'honoured the season with the old familiar carols, and have pretended there was nothing wrong'. Upon returning to France on 2 January 1916 Rayner wrote to his mother that 'I can't say I am excited at being back, but I find I have a sort of undercurrent of cheerfulness remaining from leave. It is partly tangible in the form of things I have brought back.'[19] At the end of January work for the battalion included helping the Royal Engineers to build a new railway line; February saw them return to the trenches. On 13 February Rayner wrote to his mother from No. 3 General Hospital at Le Tréport, where he was treated for a wound following fainting and pitching onto his head.

On 12 April he had to tell his mother of his disappointment in duty delaying his turn for leave, and his overwhelming fear of leave not coinciding with his brother's being at home:

> The 'bolt from the blue' has fallen, and I am off to the Front again tonight, taking some of my own men up, and also some of another unit of our division. Now it's come I am afraid I am not pleased. I had settled down to camp life and was enjoying Butland's company ... I'm afraid it makes my leave more remote, but good as Easter would be, May (which needs no June for beauty's heightening) will be better, but I must *not* miss Ed.[20]

The return of his friend John Upcott, back after recovering from his wounds sustained at Loos, did something to alleviate this disappointment. Rayner's leave was postponed again on 1 May due to giving evidence at a court martial: a fortnight later he was still writing of his disappointment at its being delayed. However, shortly thereafter he finally did get home on leave; mother and sons spent his six happy days together.

Upon returning to France and duty on 3 June Rayner duly spent Whitsun in the trenches. Then, as his letter to his mother of 22 June makes clear, preparations were under way for the Battle of the Somme, one of the bloodiest battles in human history. Optimism was the order of the day, and Rayner seemed to be at pains to reassure his mother that, as one of the most experienced soldiers in his regiment, he was not unduly worried:

> There seems to be a great confidence everywhere – I mean at home as well as in this hot-bed of optimism – that the war will be over soon, some say in July. Yesterday, for the first time, I felt it in my bones as the phrase goes, that Fritz will be strafed, distracted and destroyed. Previously I felt such awe of him I had not been able quite to see it done, though it might and was expected to be in theory ... Just fancy I have been out almost 11 months, am quite a veteran in fact; I have now seen France in each season of the circling year, and have not failed to appreciate much of it.[21]

This was followed a week later by the following letter:

> It is a small world, the latest being that our new medical officer who came to us a few days ago is one Worsley, of Pembroke College and St. Thomas' Hospital, a contemporary and friend of Ed's. Let Ed know it, it will interest him much. Upcott has not returned yet, though I have expected him for some days. I see the English papers of Monday tell of a bombardment all along our front, that is to say one we are inflicting on the German lines. As it is no secret, therefore, I can say that in our corner of the world our artillery is 'some' sight, and, even more, 'some' sound, though what I hate most about shells and all such inventions of the devil, is the bittersweet smell of unexploded crumps – a sickening smell of evil associations. Well, when the hour strikes, you can trust the Blankshires to give fits to Fritz Von Frightfulness, he will be outfrighted and outfought, so be of good cheer.[22]

On the following day Rayner sent his mother a quick note to say that in the upcoming battle he would be commanding his company, adding in parenthesis, '(Captain's work)'.[23] This was to be the last letter that Mrs Rayner ever received from her son, as on 1 July 1916 Rayner fell mortally wounded in the fighting, shot through the stomach before German lines.[24] He was 26. A heartfelt tribute to Rayner appeared in the *Pelican Record* five months after his death:

> He had a rare quality of character and a many-sided ability that made him the obvious leader of the College: and there are few men who could have carried his successes in Scholarship, in Athletics, and in College society with such an unaffected modesty, few men whose popularity had so large an element of respect.[25]

Rayner's brother Edward was killed on 9 July 1917; and their mother died in 1919. Editors of the printed letters commented that 'the family circle is again complete and unbroken'.[26]

Donald William Alers Hankey (CCC 1907–10) was born in Brighton on 27 October 1884, the fourth son of Robert Alers Hankey, who had died the year before Hankey came up to Corpus, and Helen Bakewell Hankey. He was educated at Brighton Day School and later at Rugby School from 1898 to 1901. Hankey then attended the Royal Military Academy, Woolwich from 1901 to 1903, and trained as a professional soldier. He became 2nd lieutenant in the Royal Garrison Artillery, serving in Mauritius. Hankey resigned his commission in 1907, whereupon he travelled on the Continent. He matriculated at Corpus in Michaelmas 1907 as a freshman aged 23 and was therefore older than the majority of his contemporaries, most of whom were 18 or 19. Despite this age difference, he evidently got on well with other Corpuscles and was an active member of the College, serving as Secretary and President of the Owlets. During the society's reading of *Notorious Mrs Ebbsmith* by Arthur Wing Pinero in early 1909 (a rendition deemed 'not a success'), Hankey read the part of Kirke.[27] A fortnight later, hosting the society in his own room, members of the Owlet Club read *You Never Can Tell* by George Bernard Shaw, this time apparently 'with great success'.[28] At subsequent society meetings, Hankey read the parts of Gregory in Sydney Grundy's *A Pair of Spectacles*, and Bulgin in *Strife* by John Galsworthy.[29] In November 1909, he appeared as Livens in Galsworthy's *The Silver Box*.[30] During his final exams at Corpus, Hankey obtained a second in Theology in 1910.

Hankey's life after Corpus was again varied. He travelled in British East Africa in 1910. In the following year he attended Leeds Clergy School but declined ordination. He worked for the Oxford and Bermondsey Mission in 1911–12. He then laboured in Australia until 1913, and contributed articles for the *Westminster Gazette* on disillusionment with emigrant life. Hankey apparently intended to purchase a West Australian Farm for Bermondsey Boys but the outbreak of war interrupted his plans. Three days after war was declared, Hankey 'offered himself as a recruit for Kitchener's 100,000. On the day after he enlisted he was made a corporal, and before the week was out he received the sergeant's stripes.'[31] Throughout his time in Kitchener's army in France and Belgium Hankey submitted articles on the war for *The Spectator*. These were subsequently collected and published as *A Student in Arms* in 1916, which received national success and acclaim.

In summer 1915 Hankey was persuaded by his brother of his duty to apply for a commission owing to the shortage of trained officers. He thereupon served as a sergeant in the Rifle Brigade before becoming 2nd lieutenant in the Royal Garrison Artillery and later the Royal Warwickshire Regiment. Hankey was killed in action on 12 October 1916 at Le Transloy, Morval, the Somme, and is commemorated on Thiepval Memorial. He was 31. His publications were reprinted post-humously in 1917 and 1919. The reasons for Hankey's wartime literary success have been outlined as follows:

> Hankey had no illusions about war and he never disguised the realities from his readers. His writing was valued because it offered meaning to the ordeal, not by preaching, but by showing how the 'New Armies' were actually coping with the moral and physical challenges that confronted them.[32]

The first edition of Hankey's *A Student in Arms* appeared in April 1916; it was quickly reprinted, reaching its seventeenth edition by October 1917, a year after Hankey's death.[33] Hankey's wartime experiences as part of Kitchener's army were in many ways similar to Rayner's in the Devonshire Regiment, with common themes running between the two. Certainly the two soldiers' initial attitudes before seeing pitched battle, and the difficulty in believing that they were really at war, are strikingly comparable, as seen from Hankey's letter sent to his cousin Valerie in May 1915.

> I am extraordinary glad that we did not come out before, as in this weather we have really had a splendid time, sleeping out in the long sweet grass of the meadows, and occasionally even getting a plunge in a pond, and drying oneself in the sun, which is one of the pleasantest sensations in life! Anything in more complete contrast to the sordid business of war than the manner of our life for the past ten days is difficult to imagine. It was more like a holiday camp than anything ...[34]

Likewise, reality did not take long to sink in after reaching the front:

'Finally we came to the trenches themselves, and all around was deso-lation and ruin. There are few more mournful spectacles than a town or village lately reduced to ruins.'[35]

Similarly the notion of paternalism, as in Rayner's letters, is apparent in Hankey's writings. Hankey was very critical of the attitudes of upper-class officers towards working-class soldiers. His anonymity in *The Spectator* 'freed him to rage in print at the unjust treatment of the inarticulate by his own officer class, the brutalisation of fighting men, and the hypocrisy of alternately lionising and maltreating the common soldier'.[36] Nevertheless, 'The Beloved Captain', a chapter from his *A Student in Arms*, reflects on the relationship between a popular captain and his men:

> We were his men. Already he took an almost paternal interest in us … His confidence was infectious. He looked at them, and they looked at him, and the men pulled themselves together and determined to do their best. Their best surprised themselves … We were his men, and he was our leader. We felt that he was a credit to us, and we resolved to be a credit to him … He was not democratic. He was rather a justification for aristocracy … We knew that we should lose him. For one thing, we knew that he would be promoted. It was our great hope that some day he would command the company. Also we knew that he would be killed. He was so amazingly unself-conscious. For that reason we knew he would be absolutely fearless. He would be so keen on the job in hand, and so anxious for his men, that he would forget his own danger. So it proved.[37]

Paternalism was an inescapable reality, but could, according to Hankey's experiences, sometimes be a positive influence.

One area in which Hankey's wartime writings differ strikingly from Rayner's lies in his attitude to the Church leaders of the day. Hankey 'upbraided churches for what he saw as their feeble response to the perplexity and moral confusions of the day, and for threatening hellfire to men about to face shellfire'.[38] He wrote bluntly that 'the clergy are out of touch with the laity.'[39] This was, he argued, because chaplains and wartime religious leaders failed to understand how soldiers saw their own religious convictions. Hankey was convinced that, like the officer classes who looked down on those in the ranks, Church leaders mistook soldiers' inarticulateness for a lack of religious conviction. His impatience with the Church was not caused by outright disagreement with its principles as much as frustration that its body failed to understand so many men. His disappointment 'appeared to spring from a sense of lost opportunity'.[40] Meanwhile, a further criticism of the Church – the ban on combatant service for the clergy – was aimed at both religious leaders and the country's authorities:

> The Church could be mobilized so as to set free a large number of the younger clergy, if only the leaders could see that the greatness of the opportunity made the sacrifice worth while ... A large number of older men could, if they were public-spirited enough to consent, be set free to take the place of younger men. It is being done in almost every other profession, so why not the Church? ... All that is wanted is faith from the leaders of the Church, and loyalty from the other incumbents. The younger clergy will need no pressing.[41]

This ban was lifted, in March 1918.

After initially volunteering with Kitchener's army in 1914, Hankey served in the ranks as an infantryman and later as a junior officer. He became persuaded that his pre-war professional military experience was in demand, and subsequently applied to transfer to the Warwickshire regiment. This was eventually granted in late 1915, after two months' delay. Hankey was killed in action during the later stages of the Battle of the Somme, a fortnight before his 32nd birthday. He was caught by a German machine gun, at the head of his men, leading them in a daylight charge. His battlefield grave was lost in subsequent fighting. The preface of *A Student in Arms* reflected on the phenomenal success of Hankey's wartime writing, noting that readers of *The Spectator* learned of his death 'with deep regret'. In his wartime writings, Hankey's readers had 'found consolation, interest, and delight' over the course of autumn and winter 1915 and spring 1916.

Hankey had 'proved an inspired interpreter of the private soldier' and 'was worthy to be named *liaison* officer between the nation and its Army'. The preface concluded that '"A Student in Arms" died as he wished to die – in action on the Somme'.[42] Such a memorial, jarring as it may sound to modern ears, reflects the proud and stoical obituaries that were frequently published in contemporary magazines and newspapers. These biographies, alongside cheerful letters home from soldiers on the front, should be viewed as wartime writings of equal validity with the darker poems which emerged from the battlefields. 'Intended to console and fortify, and occasionally perhaps to conceal, such letters were as authentic as the work of authors who wrote less privately, for a wider readership, and with a different point of view.'[43]

The Revd Richard William Dugdale (CCC 1908–12) was born in Salisbury on 9 November 1889, the second son of the Revd Sydney Dugdale, vicar of Lower Beeding, Sussex, and Edith Dugdale (née Marshall), who had died in 1903. He attended Rugby School for five years before following his elder brother, the Revd John Sydney Dugdale (CCC 1905–8), to Corpus as an exhibitioner in 1908. In Oxford he was Treasurer of the College's Debating Society, and achieved a second in Literae Humaniores in 1912. Afterwards, he travelled in India; he then became a curate to the rector of Holy Trinity Rugby, the Revd Claude Martin Blagden, who had previously been Assistant Chaplain at Corpus from 1907 to 1912. At Rugby, Dugdale became deacon in 1913 and priest in 1915, and shared a house with a young Rugby master. Having lost his mother when he was not quite 14, Dugdale soon became very friendly with the family of Revd W. F. Stokes, another Rugby master, addressing Mrs (Caroline) Olga Stokes as 'Mamma'. In time, with the family's blessing, Dugdale became particularly close to their elder daughter, Elinor Stokes. Almost 12 years his junior, Elinor was 13 years old when Dugdale first went out to France and was aged just 17 when he was killed. At the outbreak of war Dugdale's bishop initially refused to allow him to join up. However, after eventually obtaining permission, Dugdale served as a chaplain to the Forces in France from 1915 to 1918. Dugdale was killed in action on 23 October 1918, a mere fortnight before the Armistice. Serving as a chaplain rather than as combatant soldier, Dugdale's experiences differed from those of Rayner and Hankey, though they were evidently no less distressing. That we know so much of his time on the battlefields reflects letters written to Elinor Stokes and her mother, transcripts of which reside in the College Archives. Many of these letters reveal his growing affection for Elinor. 'His preoccupation with marriage to her, as the editor of the letters says, was to become all-consuming.'[44] The letters also serve as a poignant reminder of Dugdale's hope that he would survive the conflict, and his dreams for a happy future that he would never see.

Unlike those early letters from Rayner and Hankey, we have no letters from Dugdale describing a holiday atmosphere upon his landing in France in 1915. Indeed, upon his arrival, Dugdale was soon involved in the Battle of Loos in which most of his officer friends were killed or wounded. On 4 October, he told Mamma of his distress, tempered with reassurance: 'That is the worst part of this show – one simply can't find out anything definite about the men. However most of them are bound to turn up somewhere.'[45] A month later, Dugdale told Elinor that 'one feels here even after such a short time that one has lived among shells and broken houses for ever and ever'.[46] Perhaps partly to distract himself, and those who cared for him, from his life in France; and also out of concern for his sister, in mid-October Dugdale told Elinor that his younger sister Edith Jocelyn ('Jill') would be working as a nurse in Oxford, declaring, 'and as she is sure to feel a bit lost at first, any letters any of you write to her would be most acceptable and all that'.[47]

Dugdale's friendships were mostly restricted to close circles of Oxford and Rugby, and his letters from the front are peppered with references to Corpus friends lost or missing. In August 1916, for example, he wrote to Mamma in praise of Donald Hankey, who had been in the year above him at Corpus: 'if you want the best book yet written on the new Armies try "A Student in Arms". It is a wonderful effort.' Three days after Hankey's death on 12 October, Dugdale wrote of him again to Mamma. 'Do you see that Donald Hankey is dead? He wrote a wonderful book "A Student in Arms" – a long way the best book on the war I've seen anywhere.'[48] Then in December Dugdale asked Mamma for news of his friend William Maurice Ogle (CCC 1908–11):

> Could you find out for me what has happened to William Ogle? He was wounded in July and went to a hospital in Oxford. Somebody told me he'd died since – but I haven't seen it anywhere: and don't like to write to his wife and ask. He is a great pal of mine and I am Godfather to his son – also married him: do you remember?[49]

Happily, Ogle had not died. A professional soldier since 1911, he fought with the Queen's (Royal West Kent) Regiment. After recovering from his wounds he returned to the front to fight again. He was mentioned in despatches but was eventually placed on a retired list on account of wounds in August 1918. He later went on to become an accountant, dying in 1974. Similarly, Dugdale told Elinor on 18 August 1918 about the death of Christopher Bushell (CCC 1906–9), who had received the Victoria Cross five months previously. 'Have just seen in the Times that Kit Bushell V.C. & D.S.O. has been killed. We were at Rugby and Corpus together – he had a wife & kid: but perhaps the war will stop some day.' Dugdale's sympathy seemed particularly to extend to his friends' widows and fiancées. Despite the frustrations of being unable to formally propose to an underage Elinor, the couple seemed to find the unofficial nature of their relationship as something of a buffer in case the worst should happen, as reflected in a letter to Elinor of 1 September 1917: 'It is beastly – tho' as we always say, not so bad for you and me as it is for heaps of others.'[50]

Dugdale went on leave during autumn 1916. On 14 September he told Mamma in some distress about his fear of catching scabies from his servant, who was suffering from it, and about the measures he had taken to protect himself to ensure that it would not prevent his leave. Upon returning to France, Dugdale was subsequently transferred in late 1916, against his will, to the much less dangerous position of chaplain at an infantry officers' training school behind the lines. In a letter of 4 June 1917 he described the Infantry School as 'a jolly life but not strenuous enough for wartime'.[51] A modest man who downplayed his wartime service, it is clear that Dugdale frequently went beyond what was expected of him. On 3 March 1917, he was awarded the Military Cross for having 'tended the wounded under very heavy fire without the slightest regard for his own safety. He located wounded men in the most advanced positions and guided stretcher parties to bring them in.'[52] Moreover, his strong sense of duty made him determined never to use his role to demand privileges: he refused to ask for special leave, despite his position as a chaplain making this possible. In April 1917 he explained to Elinor that 'I cannot ask for early leave myself because it would discredit (or might do) Chaplains in general – I mean always wanting special leave etc.'[53] The year 1917 brought other hardships, as Elinor entered boarding school. Although the headmistress was Elinor's aunt, 'rules regarding visitors and outside correspondence were rigidly applied'. However, Mamma sympathised with the couple's burgeoning relationship, and 'connived by allowing a limited number of letters each term to be sent in both directions through her'.[54] A letter of mid-February, sent to Mamma, highlights the intensity of Dugdale's feelings for Elinor amongst general preparations for what became the bloody Battle of Passchendaele:

> You see it's like this – I don't want to do the pathetic, but from the Spring onwards there's going to be a show. Shows are not nice: and I personally hate them – so far it is simply the thought of the Duchesse [Elinor] that has kept me going in all the sordidness and beastliness of it. And then from time to time her letters, which are like – but if I don't stop I shall almost get poetic ... Anyhow I am most awfully badly in love with her: and almost believe she knows it, and perhaps she's in love with me too, who knows? let's talk about something else quickly.[55]

In the summer Dugdale was sent as a chaplain to the Royal Flying Corps, which eventually became the Royal Air Force (RAF). In August he was granted leave, which he spent happily with the Stokes family in Rugby. Upon returning to service, Dugdale's letters of September and October 1917 are full of accounts of tragic deaths of men and boys in accidents as well as in action. On 3 September he described the deaths of five pilots killed or missing. A fortnight later he reported that a boy had accidentally killed himself, the third fatal accident that the squadron had experienced in 16 days. In a letter written just two days later he told Elinor that another two boys had been killed that morning. Six weeks later, in a letter written to Mamma, he wrote to describe the tragic death of yet another young pilot:

> Have I written to you since the tragedy of tragedies happened? On Elinor's birthday of all days young Swann (E.A.St H – I told you about his being in one of our squadrons) was shot down in No man's land and killed – it has knocked us all very badly: he was a perfectly sweet and adorable little boy, and extraordinary loved by his whole squadron. His Major and I went up to the line to see about bringing the body back – and we buried him near his squadron. I could hardly read the service: for the first time since being out here.[56]

Thereafter, Dugdale's letters increasingly reflected his fear that he was unable truly to help the men that he was supposed to be comforting, and reported the relentlessness of death during the war which dragged on and on. In November 1917 he confessed to Mamma that he was finding things difficult. 'It isn't the strain: it's the feeling that one is not being of use to these fellows that worries me. Still one ought to go on I suppose.' In March 1918 he confessed to Elinor: 'Yes, I am war-weary, too: not that I see much war now: but I am tired of other people getting killed.'[57] He wrote for advice to the bishop who accepted his plea to once more fully share in the hardships of battalion life, and by June 1918 Dugdale was back with a battalion, the First Norfolks, alternating with six days in the line and six behind it. During that summer the Allied forces were at last advancing through German lines: leave was cancelled. Then suddenly it was allowed again, and Dugdale was granted leave in August, arriving in England before Elinor had to return to school. In writing to Elinor afterwards he described this, the last in his life, as 'the best leave we have had yet'.[58] Meanwhile, in his letter to Mamma on 13 October, Dugdale made his intentions clear:

Still the fact remains that we cannot go on much longer like this. Something definite must happen when she leaves school, either one way or the other. She will be nearly 18 then – she knows now that I hope to marry her some day, but I must be able to say so openly very soon: The situation is becoming more than I can cope with when leave comes along.[59]

Ten days later Dugdale was killed by a shell which hit the Regimental Aid Post. He died just 14 days short of the Armistice. Elinor's sorrow was raw; apparently she 'never looked seriously at another man' after Dugdale's death.[60] Dugdale's stepmother Phyllis told Mamma the following summer enclosing old letters regarding his feelings for Elinor:

I enclose dear old Dick's two letters and I can hear him arguing about it all now, he was so sweet about everything. I know it is impertinent of me to add this but my feeling is that if Elinor marries she ought never to see them, if she is unmarried at 35–40 it is her right to have them. Please forgive my interference.[61]

Elinor lived with her sister Elizabeth to be over 90, one of the thousands of women who remained unmarried because a generation of men was lost. Meanwhile, Dugdale's sister, Jill, married a Rugby master. In December 1918 she told Mamma, 'I am so thankful to have married a friend of Dick's – wouldn't it have been awful now if my husband was someone who had never known and loved him?'[62]

Corpuscles Who Came Back

Roughly three-quarters of the 382 Corpuscles who fought in the First World War returned from the front, though many did so carrying physical and psychological injuries which persisted until long after the signing of the Armistice. It is not possible to discuss all these men within the confines of this publication; and we have very little information on wounded soldiers within surviving College records, and the JCR held no meetings between June 1914 and 1919.[63] One thing we do know, however, is that aside from the 91 who were killed on service, there were also two former members who apparently died of wounds years after peace was declared in 1918. The first of these was Major Sir John Eric Birdwood Jardine (CCC 1909–13), who had read Classics at Corpus and had been active in both the Sundial Society and the Pelican Essay Club when in Oxford. He became a professional soldier in 1911 and during the First World War served in India (1914–15) and Mesopotamia (1915–19), where in 1919 he was mentioned in despatches. He became a major of the Queen's Royal West Surrey Regiment in 1921. Three years later on 24 March 1924, he died, aged 33, of gas poisoning endured while on war service in Mesopotamia.[64] The second delayed casualty was Geoffrey Herbert Wilkinson (CCC 1903–7). He, too, had read Classics at Corpus before becoming assistant master, then joint headmaster, at his father's prep school in Bayswater. During the war he served in France as lieutenant in the Hampshire Royal Garrison Artillery in 1916–18. He was invalided following a gas attack. Wilkinson died on 19 September 1933 at Sparsholt, Winchester, as a result of this wartime gassing. He was 49.[65]

Other forgotten war stories include two Corpuscles who fought for the Axis powers during the conflict. Adelbert Emil August Wahl (CCC 1890–2) was born in Mannheim, Germany, in 1872, the second son of Rudolf Frederick Wahl, industrialist, of Scheveningen, the Netherlands. He was educated at Königlich Gymnasium, Bonn, and at Corpus obtained a second in Classics Moderations in 1892, but thereafter sat no further exams and left Oxford. Instead he studied Classics, philosophy and history at the universities of Bonn, Vienna and Berlin, obtaining a DPhil from Bonn in 1895. He later became history professor at several German universities and undertook military service as reserve captain of the Uhlan Regiment, Düsseldorf, 1905–9. During the First World War he served for two years at the front as Rittmeister of Landwehr-Kavallerie. He survived the war and went on to take up the chair of history at Tübingen, from which he retired in 1937. He died in Germany in 1957.

More unusually, there was also an English-born Corpuscle who found himself fighting against the country of his birth during the war. Wilfred Henry Wells (CCC 1897–1900) was born in London in

1878 and attended Dulwich College from 1891 to 1897. At Corpus he studied Greek philosophy and history and Roman history in the Pass School, was a member of the Tenterden Essay Club, and obtained his BA in 1900. He was in Berlin by 1901, and became lecturer in English and professor at Munich University from 1909. Thereupon he took Bavarian citizenship, while remaining a British subject. When war was declared in 1914 Wells was conscripted into the Bavarian Army Labour Corps.[66] Editors of the *Pelican Record* in December 1915 reprinted an extract from the *Daily Mail* telling of Wells's plight. The 38-year-old Wells, despite being 'English in his sympathies and feeling', owed 'the discomfiture of having to take up arms against his own country to the fact that in 1909 he accepted from Munich University pension rights, which include complimentary Bavarian citizenship'. Although German–British consuls had apparently stated at the time of Wells's university employment that 'this made no difference whatever to the recipients' status as British citizens', journalists at the *Mail* supposed that Wells 'was no doubt persuaded into remaining at his post, and is now faced with a brutal alternative'.[67] No information is available on Wells after 1914 in the College *Biographical Register*, and the University did not record its past members who fought for the Axis powers in its *Roll of Service*. Thus the College and University lost track of Wells, and his fate is unknown.

Very occasionally, Corpuscles who were wounded during their military service returned to a Corpus nearly empty during the war years, to continue with their university education. Sir Ian Vincent Hamilton Campbell (CCC 1918–19) had attended Cheltenham College as a schoolboy until 1914. Thereafter instead of coming up to Corpus as planned, he served as a lieutenant in the 17th King's (Liverpool) Regiment. He fought in France and Belgium, was badly wounded at the Somme and invalided out. In the December 1916 issue of the *Pelican Record* he was erroneously listed amongst the killed; but the editors corrected this in March 1917, saying that they were 'glad to learn that he was only wounded'.[68] Campbell matriculated at Corpus during Michaelmas Term 1918. He was Secretary of the Corpus Wasps Dining Club in 1919, but thereafter left the College without sitting any University exams. Whether his wartime injuries or experiences caused him to leave early is unknown. After leaving Oxford he entered the civil service and remained there until he retired in 1955. The *Pelican Record* did make a further reference to Campbell in June 1920, announcing his forthcoming marriage to Madeline Lowe Reid [Whitelocke]: the couple were married on 4 July at St Mary Magdalen, Oxford. They went on to have one son, N. A. H. Campbell (CCC 1946–47), but Madeline died in 1929. After her death Campbell remarried twice, before dying himself in 1978.

Meanwhile, Charles Hignett (CCC 1915–16, 1918–22) was able to complete his degree after his war service. Educated at Manchester Grammar School, he matriculated at Corpus as a scholar in 1915. Thereupon he served as a gunner with the Royal Garrison Artillery, and was invalided out in 1917. In December 1917, hopeful *Pelican* editors speculated that College undergraduate numbers, then just six, might be 'restor[ed] to the mystic seven if C. Hignett is well enough to come up again'.[69] Hignett recovered enough to return to Corpus partway through 1918. He became President of the Sundial Society, won the Sidgwick Prize,[70] the University's Ireland Prize, and earned a first in Classics Moderations in 1919, before gaining a first in Literae Humaniores in 1922. He then pursued an academic career, becoming Fellow and lecturer in Ancient History at Hertford College from 1924 to 1959. He died in 1966.

Likewise, Sir Edward Hale (CCC 1917–20) arrived at Corpus with war injuries. A former pupil at Tonbridge School, Hale wrote to President Case on 7 August 1914 for advice about applying for a commission, since during his school years he 'had served nearly 6 years in the Corps, obtained Certificate "A" and reached the rank of Cadet Officer'. Five days later Hale wrote again to say that he hoped to apply for the Territorials. In November 1914 his mother sent Case a telegram informing him that her son had received a commission as 2nd lieutenant in the 7th East Lancashire Regiment, with whom he served in France until 1916.[71] Hale was wounded twice; thereafter he matriculated at Corpus in Michaelmas 1917 with his scholarship retained from three years earlier. The December 1917 edition of the *Pelican Record* offers us a rare glimpse into the extent and nature of his war injuries: 'We have also welcomed this Term in E. Hale the first of our scholars who has returned from the war, still on crutches, but ready to attack Honour Moderations as dauntlessly as he did the enemy.'[72] He was a prominent figure during the last couple of years at College, acting as Secretary of the Owlets, Secretary and President of the Pelican Essay Club, President of the Wasps, and Captain of the Boat Club. In June 1919 the *Pelican Record* wrote that 'the College owes a great debt of gratitude to E. Hale, who has re-created Corpus as a rowing College, and in spite of a disabling wound has worked wonders on the river'.[73] Hale obtained a first in Literae Humaniores in 1920 and entered the Treasury the following year, where he worked until 1950. Thereafter he was secretary of the University Grants Committee in 1951–7, before becoming administrative head of the Historical Branch of the Cabinet Office in 1958–60. He married Joan Latham [Bateson] in 1930, with whom he had two daughters. He was awarded CB in 1942 and KBE in 1952, dying in 1978.

Other Corpuscles who returned to Oxford from the war with injuries include H. S. Clemons (CCC 1919–21), who was wounded and taken prisoner of war in 1918; G. S. Facer (CCC 1919–23), also a prisoner of war 1917–18; C. S. Hall (CCC 1919–20), invalided out towards the end of the war; and E. L. Hargreaves (CCC 1919–21), wounded and taken prisoner in April 1918. C. R. S. Harris (CCC 1918–20) was invalided out in January 1918 and, in the words of the *Pelican Record*, was '"demobilized" before having a chance of paying his compliments to the enemy'.[74] J. C. E. Herold (CCC 1914–16, 1919–20) was a prisoner of war in Germany in 1918; R. G. Rees (CCC 1912–14, 1919–20) was invalided out in 1916; R. P. S. Walker (CCC 1919–20) was wounded towards the end of the war; C. M. White (CCC 1919–22) was a prisoner of war in Germany in 1917–18; E. H. Gropius (CCC 1915–20) underwent brief army service and was invalided out when his foot was crushed by an artillery wheel. Another ten undergraduates returned to Corpus after the Armistice, all of whom apparently survived the conflict without major injury. Scores more, of course, were wounded during the conflict but did not return to Corpus; we have little information on such survivors. Many did not return because they had graduated before 1914. For others, we can only speculate whether war wounds may have contributed towards decisions against returning to university after the Armistice.

A significant number of Corpuscles were decorated for their war service during the conflict. Of the 382 Corpuscles who served, 131 were decorated. Two were awarded the Victoria Cross (one posthumously). Six Corpuscles were awarded the Croix de Guerre; another two were awarded the Croix d'Officier de la Légion d'Honneur. Eight received a Distinguished Serving Order. Forty were awarded the Military Cross (one posthumously); another received the Military Medal. A further seven Corpuscles received an OBE for their military service; one was awarded a CBE; another received an MBE. A total of 52 Corpuscles were mentioned in dispatches; and nine received 'Mentions by the Secretary of State for valuable service in connexion with the War'. One Corpuscle received the Order of St Stanislas (3rd Class) (with swords); and there was a recipient of the American Distinguished Serving Medal.[75] Meanwhile a Corpus servant, A. E. Blagrove, earned a Distinguished Conduct Medal.

The 1918 influenza pandemic brought continued suffering to a world still reeling from war, and became one of the deadliest natural disasters in human history. The epidemic delayed Armistice celebrations at neighbouring Christ Church. 'With organist and choristers all laid low, celebrations had to be postponed. Instead, a commemoration service was held in the cathedral a week later.'[76] Miraculously, Corpus seemed to escape the outbreak very lightly. Nobody within the College walls died from the epidemic; but one Corpuscle evidently died as a result of influenza elsewhere. Philip Askell Benton (CCC 1898–1901) had worked in the Nigerian Civil Service after leaving Corpus, and served with the Nigerian Land Contingent during the war. He died of flu in Nigeria 11 days before the Armistice, on 31 October 1918. He bequeathed his collection of books on the Peninsular War to the College Library. Today there are 77 titles in the library containing gift notes indicating inclusion in Benton's bequest. Several of these titles are multiple volume works, and there is some indication that Corpus was originally given some 169 individual items.[77] Meanwhile, 1919 saw the death of Percival Woodcock (CCC 1919), who had served in Egypt and Salonika during the war as a private with the 79th Field Ambulance, RAMC. He matriculated at Corpus as a Scholar in Trinity Term 1919 and sat his Natural Science

Prelims. Woodcock had presumably contracted malaria during his military service, as he died of the disease at Corpus on 17 November. He was 22 years old. His obituary in the *Pelican Record* was written by a fellow war survivor, the Revd Dr Norman Henry Snaith (CCC 1917–20). Woodcock died quickly, 'having been confined to his bed for five days only'. A former pupil of Manchester Grammar School, he had enlisted as a private in the RAMC in autumn 1916 and after a preliminary training at Aldershot went out to the Near East. Stationed first near Kantara, he afterwards served for many months in the eastern desert, towards Gaza. 'There he did well – being given sole charge of the X-ray work.' Woodcock was then 'transferred to Salonika in time for the last attack, and during the final assault on the Grand Colon was well up in the firing-line, acting as stretcher-bearer'. He marched with the advancing troops up the Vardar Valley, finally reaching Rustchuk on the Danube.

> Demobilized in March of this year, he settled down compara-tively quickly. During the short time he was amongst us he did well; he gave every promise of a worthy career, and had that touch of humanness which makes the successful doctor. In the world of sport his opportunities were limited, but he was very keen, and on several occasions played in the Soccer Team. I knew him first at School in 1913 – quiet, unassuming, but with a weight of that which makes a Man. A hard worker, of a kindly heart, one of the best of friends, and one of the straightest men I have ever met. To his mother, his sister, and his brother we extend our deepest sympathy.[78]

The Corpuscle Who Refused to Fight

Despite overwhelming support for the First World War, its popularity was not universal. We saw earlier how Corpus President Thomas Case was initially very reluctant to support the conflict. Still others objected more vehemently throughout the entirety of the war. During the conflict, 16,500 British men registered as conscientious objectors and refused to undertake military service on religious or moral grounds.

Of these, 3,000 accepted non-combatant service; another 9,000 carried out various kinds of alternative service. This left 1,300 'absolutists', men who accepted prison sentences as a witness to their opposition to war.[79] One of these absolutists was the Corpuscle Thomas Simons Attlee (CCC 1899–1902), elder brother of future prime minister Clement Attlee.

Attlee was born in Putney on 18 October 1880, the sixth among the eight children of Henry Attlee, solicitor, and Ellen Bravery (née Watson). He attended Haileybury School in Hertfordshire before coming to Corpus to read Modern History, obtaining a second in 1902. Afterwards he trained as an architect, becoming an associate of the Royal Institute of British Architects in 1907. In 1913 he married Kathleen Ida Mary (née Medley), a Charity Organization Society social worker and member of Poplar Council. The couple went on to have two sons born during the war. Following the outbreak of war, the eldest Attlee sibling, Bernard, enlisted as a military chaplain. The seventh sibling, Clement, went out of his way to serve. At 31, he was already over the age limit for new recruits and was initially refused a commission, and it was only at the very end of September that he was commissioned with the 6th South Lancashire Regiment, later known as the Prince of Wales's Volunteers. Meanwhile the youngest sibling, Laurence, volunteered to join Kitchener's army. 'It was thus that the two youngest Attlee children, born into the self-confident world of late Victorian Britain, ended up on the blood-soaked beaches of Gallipoli.'[80] As a committed Christian and pacifist Thomas Attlee opposed the war on religious grounds; and when conscription was introduced in 1916 he steadfastly refused to fight. On 22 January 1917 he was arrested and appeared in court on the following day, charged with being an absentee under the Military Service Act. A report published in the *East London News and Chronicle* stated that upon his arrest Attlee had said, 'I am a conscientious objector. I don't intend to appear for service. I'll go the whole hog or none. I have been offered non-combatant service but I won't have it.'[81] He spent the next few weeks in the hands of the military; he was court-martialled and sentenced to three months in prison.

We have a good understanding of Attlee's stance against warfare owing to a detailed letter that he sent his sister Margaret ('Midge') during summer 1916. In this letter, Attlee wrote of his belief that pacifism was the 'central fact' of Jesus's life and teaching, and that Christians should thus emulate these lessons: 'He declined what was a patriotic thing to do – to fight for a just cause against oppression – because His whole teaching was that that is not the way.' Jesus told us not only to 'Love your neighbours' but also to 'Love your enemies', and Attlee found such teachings especially relevant to a war-torn world because Jesus had brought His commands 'right down into our present imperfect world, where we still make enemies in spite of the advice to love our neighbours'. Attlee argued that in 1914 a small minority of militarists across Europe had been able to convince their fellow countrymen that they found themselves in danger from international aggressors, and that war was thus a regrettable but reasonable act of self-defence. Presented with such arguments, wrote Attlee, 'the whole mass of peaceable people will be driven to rally to their support and will support them through any atrocities as long as that danger exists'. If Russia had refused to mobilise, he declared, 'the Prussian militarists could not have stampeded the German people into supporting them "to ward off a Russian invasion"'. If, in turn, Germany had refused to mobilise, 'neither the French nor the English peoples would have sanctioned an attack on her'. When Britain declared that, in the event of war, she would go against Germany, Germany found herself attacked not only on her eastern and southern borders, but also from the west. Thus Attlee described Germany's occupation of Belgium as '*essential to the very existence* of the nation that "justified" that unjustifiable step to the mass of the German people'. What was wanted at this point, Attlee believed, was 'some obviously disinterested act' to stop the build-up to war in its tracks. Attlee did not see war as a bad solution to international disagreement; rather he declared that 'war is not a *worse* way – *it is no way at all*'.

Attlee believed that Jesus's doctrine of pacifism was not just a powerful example which Christians should follow, but was also one of 'hard common sense': only through refusing to resort to violence could there be any hope of success. Attlee asked pointedly, 'when has war ever "settled" anything?' He argued that embarking on war had not saved Belgium; rather she had been 'devastated from end to end' through violence. He wrote that Britain's Entente with France had sacrificed the Belgian people because Britain had not promised to attack whichever country invaded Belgium. In effect, Britain had told Germany, 'if there's a war we shall come in against you anyhow and if you enter Belgium it will only make us more determined'. Furthermore, Attlee could see no positive outcome for the world when the violence ended, even if the Allied forces emerged victorious, because the war's winners and losers would need to live alongside each other, something which would be even more difficult to do after years of bloodshed:

> And suppose we win, suppose we do thoroughly beat Germany. There are only two courses to pursue – either to kill off all the Germans *en masse* or *to live with them as neighbours*. And (as in a private quarrel) we're faced with exactly the same problem as we had to solve at first – how to get the 'better self' of Germany on top. We're handicapped by hatred of Germany – appalling hatred – and how can they believe our bonafides?

Germany, he wrote, would have good reason to be sceptical of Britain's peacetime impartiality since in the course of the war she laid claim to Germany's colonies and had boasted of capturing German trade. Attlee concluded with his firm belief that 'war doesn't work: to kill one devil you call up seven new ones'.[82]

Attlee was imprisoned in Wormwood Scrubs at the start of 1917. The sentence for conscientious objectors was relentless, with enforced silence and solitude. Accordingly, Attlee spent the first month of his sentence in solitary confinement, during the first two weeks of which he slept on a plank without a mattress and on a diet of bread and water. Later, gruel and potatoes were added to his diet, and eventually fat bacon or suet, beans or occasionally meat. Prisoners had to rise at 5.30am, eat their evening meal at 4pm and suffered lights out at 8pm. Otherwise, aside from half an hour of exercise in the yard, prisoners, after cleaning their cells and 'slopping out', had a quota of work to fulfil, usually sewing mailbags or coalsacks. After the first month, work was done 'in association' in the workshop, but no talking was permitted at any time: even with wardens, only 'necessary' conversation was allowed. Meanwhile, all writing was strictly forbidden; and the rules about letters were precise. Generally, prisoners could write no letter for up to two months following their incarceration. Subsequently, letters extending to three-quarters of a page were permitted monthly, and one letter and a photograph could be received. Unsurprisingly, the poor diet, isolation, silence, continual observation, and lack of trust and often abusive treatment by the wardens 'put a great strain on all the prisoners'.[83]

On 14 July 1917 Attlee was released and was sent to the barracks at Frimley, Surrey, where he was attached to the 3/10th London Regiment. He was permitted to receive a few visitors, but it wasn't long before another court martial gave him a second sentence, this time for a year, which he served in Wandsworth Prison. Again, he spent the first month of his sentence in isolation. By early 1918 Attlee had completed his first year of imprisonment and was eligible for some of the concessions which had been won for conscientious objectors through a hard-fought campaign waged in parliament by the small group of sympathetic members, Quakers and the Independent Labour Party. Chief among these concessions was 'a right to more reading matter, when this was available; to one short letter a fortnight instead of one long one per month; to wear their own clothes instead of one-size rough garments and to have two exercise periods per day *with conversation* – not on current events'.[84] Apparently this year-long sentence was slightly reduced, as on 26 March 1918 Attlee was temporarily released and was again able to receive visitors and exchange letters. Peggy Attlee, his biographer and daughter-in-law, notes that two letters from his brother Clem have survived from this period, though doubts whether they brought him much comfort:

> Apart from expressing, in both letters, his contempt for the Church of England and for religion generally, Clem was clearly quite unable to understand or appreciate Tom's pacifism. For Clem, force had to be met with force; the present struggle was one of white against black, and 'he who wills the end must will the means'.[85]

Shortly afterwards, Attlee received a third prison sentence, which his biographer notes that he accepted 'with remarkable equanimity'.[86] Although the Armistice was declared on 11 November 1918, there was a delay in releasing conscientious objectors from prison. There were, of course, large numbers of soldiers to be demobilised and 'it was not considered politic to set COs free while conscripts were still under orders'.[87] Early 1919 saw various petitions asking for their release; and eventually it was decided that all those who, like Attlee, had served two years or more should be released in April. Attlee was finally discharged from the army 'for misconduct' on 8 April 1919, after two years and 76 days. He re-joined his family two days later. His brother Clem, meanwhile, had fallen ill while on active service in France in October 1918; he was sent back to England to recover, and was able to leave the army almost immediately after the Armistice. Their mother, Ellen Attlee, was said to have declared, 'I don't know which of these two sons I am more proud of.'[88] Thomas Attlee's elder son, Christopher Sebastian Bravery Attlee (CCC 1934–7), eventually followed his father to Corpus in 1934, becoming the Secretary and later President of the Sundial Society, and obtained a third in Modern History in 1937. He undertook military service during the Second World War, serving as a 2nd lieutenant with the Royal Army Service Corps on the British Solomon Islands. Thomas Attlee himself undertook Red Cross and Civil Defence work during the conflict. Attlee died on 11 October 1960, a week before his 80th birthday.

Conscientious objectors were often deeply unpopular with the majority of their contemporaries, scorned as 'cowards' and 'traitors'. This poem by Sidney Olivier (CCC 1877–81), 'To conscientious objectors, on the approach of peace', appeared in the June 1919 issue of the *Pelican Record*, a testimony to the complicated but generally critical sentiments that were frequently levelled towards such men:

You were not our best-favoured. – They are slain.
All the bright youth in whom God's word of man
Most visibly was made flesh snatched arms and ran,
Clear-sighted, to man's rescue. You remain:–
For you knew better – knew their agony vain,

Their offering delusions – knew God's plan
For man's deliverance since the world began, –
The saints' sure refuge in an age insane.
Now comes your trial. Now that the brute is bound,
Quelled solely through their faith and sacrifice,
What is your part? What service shall be found
That England will allow you? I surmise
You will not be much beloved: but it must be
You are saved to us for something. We shall see.[89]

Yet conscientious objectors 'made a name for themselves and by
their persistence and steadfastness won respect even from many who
disagreed completely with their views'.[90] When, a generation later,
the Second World War broke out, Britain had 66,000 conscientious
objectors, four times as many as during 1914–18. In his autobiograph-
ical *Short Journey*, published during the course of the Second World
War, Sir (Ernest) Llewellyn Woodward (CCC 1908–11, Honorary
Fellow 1960–71) wrote that, 'as time went on, I began to dislike more
and more the celebration of Armistice Day. I wished that all the formal
ceremonies might be abandoned, and that this commemoration of the
dead could be left to those for whom it had some personal meaning.'[91]
In the eye of history, Attlee appears less out on a limb than he must
have seemed to his contemporaries.[92]

3

CORPUS SERVANTS IN WARTIME

Servants Who Fought and Died

During the First World War Corpus's servants suffered a 12.5 per-cent death rate. Of the 16 servants who fought, two were killed at the front. While there is less material to be found on these individuals in College records than on their undergraduate contemporaries – College staff are listed in neither the *Biographical Register* nor *War Service* – we are still able to get sketches, sometimes detailed sketches, of their lives at College and their wartime deaths. Material is particularly rich on the two servants who died in the war: Alfred Clifford and Henry George Ward.

Alfred William Clifford was born on 12 November 1894 and was baptised ten days later in Jericho's St Barnabas church. He was the ninth of 12 children – 11 of whom survived into adulthood – of Walter Clifford, labourer, gardener and bricklayer, and Catherine Loveday (née Walker). The Clifford family lived at 7 Mount Street in Jericho. At the start of the 20th century, Walter Clifford worked as a printer's labourer, possibly at the nearby Oxford University Press, and, like many of their neighbours, the family relied on the local printing trade for employment. Early in 1913 Alfred's father took on the licence of the Running Horses, a boatmen's and bargees' pub on the corner of Hythe Bridge Street and Fisher Row, and the family moved there as a result. However, Walter died only a few months later, in July 1913, aged 52; his widow, Catherine, then aged 49, moved with her remaining children to 28 Alexandra Road off the Botley Road.[1]

According to the 1911 census, 17-year-old Alfred worked as a printer's apprentice; but sometime between 1911 and the outbreak of war, he left the printers to work at Corpus. College sources record neither the date at which Alfred Clifford began his employment nor his job title; but the December 1914 edition of the *Pelican Record* lists Clifford among Corpus servants serving at the front.[2] He enlisted and served with the 5th Battalion of the Oxfordshire and Buckinghamshire Light Infantry (OBLI), a battalion formed at Oxford in August 1914 in response to Lord Kitchener's call for 100,000 volunteers. Clifford's older brother Ernest was already in the regular army, and his younger brother Bernard also later enlisted in Oxford, eventually becoming a private in the 25th Company of the Machine Gun Corps.[3]

Clifford's battalion landed at Boulogne in May 1915. In the December 1915 issue of the *Pelican Record* he was listed as 'missing',[4] and his death is recorded in the magazine's June 1916 issue.[5] We know, however, that Alfred was killed on 25 September 1915, aged 21, taking part in the assault on Bellewaarde Farm, east of Ypres, a subsidiary attack in support of the Battle of Loos which began in Artois that day. His body was never recovered, but he is commemorated on the Menin Gate at Ypres. Clifford's name is also inscribed on the Corpus war memorial, and on the Osney First World War memorial in St Frideswide's church on the Botley Road. The St Frideswide's church memorial lists 82 names and was unveiled and dedicated on Easter Day 1922. Alfred's younger brother Bernard is also named there, as he was killed in action in Belgium on 31 July 1917, aged 20. Sometime after the end of the war their mother Catherine (who never remarried after the death of her husband) moved to 5 Mayfair Road in Cowley and died in 1946 aged 83, in the Radcliffe Infirmary.[6]

More is known of Henry George Ward, Corpus's second servant killed during the conflict. Ward was born during summer 1898 in Marston, then a village two miles to the north-east of Oxford city centre (now known as Old Marston, it became part of the city in 1991). Named after his father, he was the youngest of four children

of Henry George Ward, gardener, and Emily (née Knibbs).[7] In March
1903 Ward's father was appointed as a gardener at Corpus: referred to
in College records as 'George' Ward, he worked at Corpus throughout
the war, and was evidently still working there in November 1918.[8]

From the 1911 census we know that Henry's 19-year-old sister
Emily had by then left home and was working as a live-in servant
for the Hatt family at Church Farm, Elsfield; as for his brothers,
17-year-old Cecil and 15-year-old Ernest, they were both working
as florists' errand boys.[9] Henry himself was then still at school; but
on 10 September 1912, aged 14, he accompanied his father and was
appointed as a servant at Corpus. His role was that of assistant or
'boy' for Charlie Bancalari,[10] a 23-year-old College servant, who went
on to work as SCR butler for many years until he retired in 1948.[11]

Henry Ward worked at Corpus for two or three years, but in 1914
or 1915, when he was only 16 or 17, he joined the 1/4th Battalion of
the OBLI, serving as a private. Ward must have lied about his age, as
men were supposed to be 18 to enlist and 19 to be sent to the front.
The battalion was sent to the Somme and Ward was killed in action
on 23 July 1916, at the Battle of Pozières, aged just 17, making him
Corpus's youngest wartime casualty. He was buried at the Pozières
British Cemetery at Ovillers-La Boisselle; at the request of his father
his gravestone was inscribed, 'He hath done what he could'. As well as
appearing on the Corpus war memorial, Ward is commemorated on
the war memorial in St Nicholas church, Old Marston. This memorial
features 12 names and was dedicated on 7 December 1919. Ward's
brother Ernest is also named on the St Nicholas church memorial: he
served as a corporal in the 2/4th Battalion of the OBLI and was killed
in action on 21 March 1918, aged 21. Ward's father died in September
1939, aged 73. He was buried in St Nicholas churchyard and his widow,
Emily, arranged for the following words to be added to his gravestone:
'also his sons, Ernest Alfred 1918 and Henry George 1916, both killed
in France'. Emily died in 1941, aged 69, and was buried with her
husband.[12]

Servants Who Fought and Survived

Another 14 servants from Corpus served at the front during the First World War and survived. Records on these individuals are patchy at best, but nonetheless something is known of them and their experiences.

William Balk, born in 1894, was the youngest of the four children of Charles and Mary Balk. He was appointed as a servant at Corpus on 14 October 1913. Employed as a pastry cook for an annual wage of £30, he was contracted to work for three nine-week terms a year.[13] Such tenure was not unusual: certainly before the 1930s scouts were '"released" by the Colleges during the Long Vacation and found their living at holiday hotels' across the country.[14] At the outbreak of war, Balk clearly enlisted early for war work, as the December 1914 edition of the *Pelican Record* notes that he was one of five College servants already serving in the war: 'W. Baulk [Balk], Pastrycook in the College kitchen, has joined the Royal Navy permanently in the same capacity.'[15] Balk served in this way throughout the war. Subsequent editions of the *Pelican Record* refer to his position as a pastry cook with the Royal Navy. Within the College Archives proper, however, nothing more is mentioned of him until the Servants' Committee meeting of 2 September 1919, when the committee noted that they would 'offer Balk £80 and food in Term, and failing him £80 for a new cook'.[16] It is unclear whether Balk accepted this offer, as this is the last time he appears by name within College records.

Arthur Edward Blagrove, as we have seen, was keen to enlist following the outbreak of war, but was initially dissuaded from doing so by President Case's reluctance to promise to keep his College job available upon return. Blagrove, 'son of University Verger', was appointed as under porter at Corpus on 15 February 1909, aged 21. Four and a half years later, in October 1913, the Servants' Committee minutes note that he was appointed 'bedmaker, in place of W. Wills (Pensioned off) from the commencement of 1914 at £40 a year and 6 Undergraduates including Room No 9'. An annotation to the minutes reads, 'it is to be pointed out to Blagrove that he has no right to Supper after Hall Dinner, the continuance of which may be reconsidered and that he can claim no compensation.'[17] Blagrove had thus just been in his new post at Corpus for about eight months when war was declared in August 1914. Following the Governing Body meeting of 10 October, in which it was officially decided that the College would do everything in its power to assist in the war effort, Blagrove and other servants were given the assurance that, should they decide to enlist, every effort would be made to ensure that their College jobs would be kept open for them upon their return. Such an assurance sufficed for Blagrove to sign up: in the *Pelican Record* of December 1914 he is listed as a member of the College servant body in military service.[18] Blagrove volunteered with the RAMC, with which he served throughout much of the war. By June 1918, however, he had reached the rank of sergeant major in the Cadet Corps; moreover he had been awarded the Distinguished Conduct Medal for his war service.[19] Sadly, we have no news of Blagrove following the end of the war. His name does not appear in any of the Servants' Committee minutes, so it seems unlikely that he returned to Corpus after the Armistice. His post-war fate, therefore, remains a mystery.

Percy Cross was born in 1884, and began working as a servant at Corpus on 12 February 1904.[20] In March 1905 he was promoted from his previous position of Common Room assistant to under butler, replacing a previous servant called William Wilsdon who had recently been dismissed 'owing to drunkenness and inattention to duty'. Early in 1914 Cross apparently applied for higher wages as a result of private family difficulties; this application was rejected by the Servants' Committee during a meeting on 21 February, but the College agreed instead to 'grant him a Donation of £5 in consequence of illness of his Wife and extra expenses'.[21] Cross clearly did not enlist following the outbreak of war in summer 1914, but evidently volunteered or was conscripted two years later. In June 1916 the *Pelican Record* noted that Cross was serving with the Yeomanry[22] and by June 1917 he was serving with the OBLI.[23] Cross returned to Corpus after the Armistice, and in a meeting of the Servants' Committee in April 1919 it was decided that, returning to his previous position of under butler, Cross was to be paid £2 a week.[24] Cross remained a popular figure within College; many years later, he was remembered fondly in reminiscences as 'Mr. Cross, who kept the College silver immaculate, and held court in the buttery with his engaging conversation. He would sometimes discuss members of the College not present at the time, occasionally delivering the considered verdict "Ah, Mr So-and-so, he's a *gentleman*"'.[25]

Meanwhile, while we know that Charles Hore started working at Corpus on 22 February 1909,[26] his role within College is unrecorded, although in the 1911 census his occupation is listed as 'College Grocer's Man'. However, by June 1916 he was listed in the *Pelican Record* as being a College servant in military service.[27] During the conflict Hore served with the OBLI (Territorial Force), in the Reserve Battalion. Following the Armistice and demobilisation, Hore returned to Corpus and took up, or resumed, duties as a groundsman, and was praised for his 'unremitting labour' in tackling College sports grounds – thought to be a 'hopeless' job – 'with cheerful perseverance'.[28]

We have very little information regarding six other College servants who undertook military service during the First World War. Frederick Milligan, born 1870, was serving with the OBLI by March 1917;[29] but aside from this we know nothing of his life and work at Corpus. There was also an L. Moore amongst the College servants who served with the RAMC from 1916.[30] Horace Mundy had enlisted with the OBLI (Territorial Force) by the end of 1915.[31] A. Reeve, meanwhile, was a sergeant with the 3rd Royal West Kent Regiment within a year and a half of the outbreak of war.[32] College servant Frank Shrimpton undertook military service with Motor Transport from 1916.[33] Finally, P. West was serving with the Royal Navy by June 1915.[34]

As well as very youthful College servants undertaking military service, older servants seem to have been keen to assist with the war effort. One Robert Scragg in College employ is a case in point. In September 1909 Scragg had been superannuated as College servant on Bancalari's staircase and was replaced by one Percy Walker. Then in January 1914 the Servants' Committee reappointed Scragg as an under porter. The minutes from the meeting note that there had been 33 applicants, of whom three, including Scragg, were selected. It was decided that his wages were to begin at £45 a year, and he 'was warned that he had no right to Supper after Hall and that if it was discontinued he must not expect compensation'. A further note records that Scragg had been, for the last four years, an under servant at University College, and had previously worked at Corpus as a boy under Bancalari Senior.[35] Following the outbreak of war in summer 1914, Scragg was clearly keen to serve his country. By December the *Pelican Record* noted that he was serving with the RAMC in Oxford,[36] with which he remained throughout the war. Following the Armistice and restoration of peace, Scragg made two final interesting appearances in the College Servants' Committee papers in June 1919: 'Scragg late Under Porter having been demobilised, but unable to sleep in College for domestic reasons in the future, he cannot return to his former post, but should a vacancy occur, his case to be considered as a possible College Servant.' Scragg, by now in his 60s, was evidently struggling with the practical requirements required for an under porter, but was clearly keen to return to employment at Corpus if possible. Just over a week later the committee decided: 'C. Bancalari to have offer of Staircases Nos 7, 8 and 10 but to have definite reply from him by July 7th whether he will return or not. If C.B. does not return Scragg to have offer of these Staircases. All on monthly agreement.'[37] It is evident from the Servants' Committee minutes, however, that Scragg never did return to Corpus; what became of him after being demobilised in 1919, therefore, is not known.

Another servant to undertake war service was William Turner. First appointed at Corpus as under porter on 7 October 1907, Turner was subsequently listed as the College's messenger in February 1909. Two years later he was planning to marry, as on 23 March 1911 he was given permission to do so by the Servants' Committee (the post of College messenger seems to have been traditionally held by a bachelor).[38] As messenger, Turner was responsible for delivering the post several times a day, but he could also be asked (and be paid) to 'polish boots and even to buy theatre tickets besides; before the First World War Colleges rarely had their own Junior Common Room and never telephones, so that the young men lived, worked and played in their own rooms, sending written notes to each other two or three times a day'.[39] Shortly after the outbreak of war Turner, like Scragg, enlisted for war service with Oxford's RAMC.[40] The *Pelican Record* notes his service with them throughout the war, and Turner's last mention within College records is in the December 1918 issue of the same magazine as serving with the RAMC.[41] Thereafter his name disappears from College records, and his post-war fate is unknown.

We know slightly more about a further College servant who undertook military action during the First World War: F. E. Williams. Fred Williams served in several roles at Corpus early in the 20th century. His name first appears in the Servants' Committee minutes on 1 May 1903, when he was appointed Corpus under porter. A little over four years later he became a bedmaker within College. By 1911 Williams had become a servant of Staircase 12, but by the end of 1913 he was again listed as a bedmaker, staircase unspecified.[42] It appears that Williams remained within the College's employ during the early years of the war, but by summer 1916 he had been conscripted and was serving with the Yeomanry, staying for about a year.[43] By June 1917, however, he was serving with the OBLI, where he remained until the end of the war.[44] Following his demobilisation, Williams returned to Corpus in spring 1919 and resumed work on staircases in the Gentlemen Commoners' Building and Kitchen.[45] Thereafter his name ceases to appear in College records; presumably he left Corpus later and found work elsewhere.

One final Corpus servant to fight in and survive the Great War was Joseph Young. Sometime during the early 20th century Young, born in about 1886, was employed as a 'boy' or assistant to one Mr Sallis, a bedmaker at Corpus. In February 1905 the Servants' Committee decided that Young was to be 'allowed to remain, although over 19, until end of Summer Term 1905'. Evidently following his 'outgrowing' of this position in mid-1905 Young found employment elsewhere in College, as by June 1910 he was serving as Corpus Common Room boy. His name appears again in the minutes of October 1914 under a list of servants to receive compensation following the decision by the Servants' Committee to discontinue supper after Hall during term; following the outbreak of war and the emptiness of College buildings, clearly this was thought no longer feasible. It was decided that Young (and another ten servants) would receive 4*d*. a night for eight weeks.[46] Young remained a servant of the College during the early stages of the war, before joining the OBLI, with which he served from late 1916 until the end of the war.[47] He does not seem to have returned to Corpus thereafter, so what became of him after the war ended is unknown.

Servants Who Remained at Corpus During the War

While the information that we have on servants who fought during the war is patchy, records regarding the servants who remained are patchier still. Although the College kept minute books of meetings held by the Servants' Committee during the early 20th century, the notes made therein are very brief, sparse in detail, and do not record the names of all those on the staff. While Fellows and undergraduates are listed in the College *Biographical Register* from 1880, servants are not included in these volumes. Similarly the *Pelican Record*, while recording the College's academic and extracurricular events, hardly ever refers to domestic matters. So we know very little indeed about the people who worked at Corpus throughout the war and laboured to keep it running and habitable for the few residents who lived there. However, we can catch occasional glimpses of them.

The March 1914 issue of the *Pelican Record* makes a very rare reference to College servants:

> Wills, who used to have staircases eight and ten, has had to retire after a rather serious illness, and his place has been taken by Blagrove, who was formerly junior porter. In his place Robert Scragge [sic] has come, whom some former members of the College may remember as the boy who used to assist the elder Bancalari on staircases four and five. The latter is now in charge of the New Buildings in place of Bunce, who retired three or four years ago.[48]

Thus we learn that there was something of a shake-up of Corpus's domestic arrangements in the months before the outbreak of war. From the Servants' Committee minutes we know that William Henry Wills had been employed as a bedmaker at Corpus since at least 1901.

At a meeting in October 1913 the committee noted that: 'W. Wills Bedmaker fell down in a fit the 3rd in 10 months. Bursar to see his Doctor as it was not considered safe and advisable to go on supporting him. If sent away to have 7/6 a week Pension and to be repaid the amount he has paid towards his Life Insurance.'[49] Just over a fortnight later it was decided that Wills, who was in his early 50s, was not well enough to work, and he was pensioned off. Blagrove, formerly under porter, was appointed in Wills's stead from the beginning of 1914, to be responsible for half-a-dozen undergraduates' rooms. It was also decided that, for the present at least, Mr Bancalari, with the assistance of a 'boy' (possibly 15-year-old Henry Ward), was to continue as Mr Phelps's servant. Here, a note in parenthesis reads, 'the Bursar raised the difficulty of 2 Servants working on One Staircase, as a serious question; and one in his opinion fraught with danger.'[50] What this possible 'danger' was is not clear; but perhaps the worry was that having two servants working in different capacities on one staircase – presumably Mr Phelps's room was located here – would be inefficient or lead to the servants spending an excessive time socialising rather than working. The issue does not appear again in the Servants' Committee papers: presumably either the arrangement did not cause the problems that the Bursar envisaged, or else it was a temporary arrangement only, and more permanent arrangements were fixed without being recorded in the minutes.

The next major decisions decided upon by the Servants' Committee recorded in the minute book occurred almost a year later, after the outbreak of war. In October 1914, as we have already seen, the committee decided to discontinue servants' supper after Hall, and compensate the individuals affected accordingly with 4d. every evening during term time.[51] The next decision, made about a month later, affected everyone on the staff much more significantly:

> In consequence of the War and consequent great decrease in the number of Undergraduates in residence, it was decided that the Bursar was to give every servant in College 3 months notice from the 9th of November, as a precautionary measure. Note for Bursary: Some new arrangement will be made suitable to the

circumstances but this might necessitate the removal of some of the servants.[52]

Corpus, practically emptied of its student body and housing only a limited number of Fellows, required only a skeleton staff to keep the College running throughout the war. A few individuals were retained during the early years of the war – at the very least, the kitchen remained in use, a small number of rooms were still occupied, and someone was needed to man the Lodge – but the names and posts of those individuals were not recorded. Thereafter, on 21 November 1914, Corpus Governing Body made two relevant resolutions. Firstly, College servants' pay during military absence 'should be such that with the Army pay and allowances the College will not allow the servant to lose', as long as he came 'under the same deductions, if any, from wages as the other servants'. Secondly, a servant would be reinstated and, if desired, assigned to work 'so far as possible of the same character as that now performed by him, provided that he is discharged for military service with a good character and sound in health'.[53] Thus we know the College's decisions regarding wartime servants away on military service; but any decisions or policies made regarding the few individuals who remained during the early years of the war are not known to us.

After a silence of 18 months the Servants' Committee met again in May 1916, shortly after the enforcement of the Military Service Act which introduced conscription of men between 18 and 41. Several Corpus servants not already in military service were soon called up, requiring the College to find replacements from elsewhere. Thus it was that, following the call-up of the under porter, Corpus waterman George Best was employed in his stead at a salary of £1. 15s. a week, at a rate of £1. 7s. 6d. to the College and 7s. 6d. to the Undergraduate Clubs.[54] Born in 1861, Best had been appointed waterman from a riverside family in 1879. A popular, respected and well-known figure within College, he was said to have 'ruled the Boat Club with a rod of iron', and continued to do so until he died in 1935.[55] The lack of rowing on the river – OTC exercises aside, very few student clubs functioned during wartime – must have made him an obvious choice to assist with work elsewhere within College. At the same meeting it was announced that, following the call-up of the under butler, Griffin would assist in the Buttery during his absence at a salary of 14s. a week; Chandler would clean knives for 2s. 6d.; and George Brooks would attend to hot plates at 2s. 6d. per week.[56] Biographical information on these individuals is harder to come by. However, in 1905 Edward Chandler, then holding the position of bootblack, had been given permission to marry,[57] so he must have been in College employment for over a decade; while George Brooks had been working as bedmaker since at least 1904,[58] and so was also well known to the College.

At the next recorded Servants' Committee meeting in December 1917, decisions were made about servants' wartime wages. 'Some of the College Servants having asked for a rise in Wages owing to the War prices it was unanimously decided not to give a rise in Wages, but to grant a War Bonus for 1917.'[59] This was followed by a detailed list of wages for each individual, broken down to list both regular salary and payment for extra work and responsibilities during wartime. Thus we know the names of the individual servants at Corpus throughout the third year of the war, and occasionally we also know their role. Hence we learn that George Brooks, who under usual circumstances worked as a bedmaker, undertook additional wartime assistance in the Buttery. Walter John Sallis, meanwhile, was a long-standing servant who worked as a bedmaker on an unspecified staircase within Corpus (previously assisted by Joseph Young until summer 1905, and by E. Hunt in 1907). Joseph Colborn, listed as a bedmaker in 1901, was evidently still working at Corpus in 1917. Meanwhile, Percy Bancalari was a long-standing servant of Corpus, having been appointed by the College on 6 December 1899;[60] but since his brother Charlie, his father, his wife, and possibly his son were also at some time in the College's employ, and rarely are any of them distinguished by a first initial within the Servants' Committee minutes, so it is difficult to tell them apart within the records. Charlie Bancalari was appointed in Percy's place on staircases 4, 5 and 9 on 23 August 1910; what is less clear is which role exactly Percy then took up, but he evidently remained working elsewhere in College. In 1917 Percy was paid a total of £140; this was made from his regular College wages and fees alongside earnings for wartime Lodge duty and work in the Common Room, a war bonus, and £17 in rent (his usual role, clearly, required him to live on site). Meanwhile William Bancalari (presumably his son or some other relation), the College Buttery boy since Michaelmas 1913, was paid 14s. a week during vacation and 19s. during term, and received a war bonus of £5. Charlie Bancalari, however, is missing from this particular set of accounts.

From the 1917 list of servants' wages, we also know that Henry Coombes, Corpus Senior Common Room man who had first arrived at the College aged 14 in the 1850s,[61] was still on the staff in the same capacity in 1917; and that the Corpus porter was Frederick Wilsdon (appointed 10 June 1899).[62] Meanwhile Mr Knibbs (appointed Corpus manciple on 25 March 1907)[63] was assisted in the kitchen by one Thomas Luckett, recorded as Corpus cook in 1904. Mrs Mott, whose role in College is not specified, received weekly wages of 10s. Edward Chandler, the bootblack who also assisted in the kitchen cleaning knives during the war, received regular weekly wages alongside additional wages from the College Rugby Football Club. Similarly, the boatman and wartime under porter George Best continued to receive weekly wages from both the College and the Clubs. George Ward, Corpus gardener since 1903, whose 17-year-old son had been killed at the Somme, was working part-time by 1917. In addition Mrs Predell continued to receive her weekly pension from Corpus; then in her 80s, she had retired from College employment in mid-1912. The Servants' Committee minutes record: 'Mrs Predell lately employed on Staircases Fellows Buildings I and II to receive a Pension of 3/– a week after 23 years' service. Now aged 74. In the meantime at any rate the Servants on Staircases I and II as above to do with a Woman servant.'[64] The final College servant listed in the 1917 war wages records is J. A. Goldsworthy. Appointed by the College on 23 April 1901,[65] he was listed in 1904 as the College clerk, but from January 1910 was Corpus butler. It seems that, during the war at least, Goldsworthy was employed in both capacities.[66]

The next Servants' Committee meeting took place six months later, in June 1918, during which there were four items on the agenda, all implying that many College employees were struggling to make ends meet during a period of rising living costs. It was decided that bedmaker Joseph Colborn, now approaching 60, would be allowed to take work outside Corpus after 9 o'clock in the morning during the Long Vacation, subject to the Bursar's approval. An additional note reads, 'if any difficulty arises he can go on his Pension.' Likewise it was decided that Walter Sallis, now in his mid-50s, would be allowed to take outside work during the Long Vacation if he wished, on the same terms as Colborn. Lack of a young male workforce during wartime meant that there was a surfeit of work available to older and female workers. By permitting employees to work elsewhere alongside undertaking College duties, Corpus continued to demonstrate its willingness to assist in the war effort as best it could. Thirdly, Luckett, the cook, was to receive £80 a year in wages (rather than £60). Similarly, Mrs Mott found her weekly wages raised from 10s. to 13s. during the Long Vacation.[67]

Stagnant nominal wages and rising prices continued to plague Corpus and its staff as the war dragged on. As 1918 drew to a close, the Servants' Committee called a final wartime meeting in order to agree upon recommendations for servants' wages to take to the Governing Body meeting on 9 November. The committee laid out a detailed list of servants' wages for 1914, 1917 and 1918, and a list of 'extras existing',[68] which consisted mainly of individuals' meals provided by the College. The total annual wages of the servants were calculated by the Servants' Committee to be £1,135. 5s. in 1914, £1,295 in 1917 and £1,450 in 1918, a nominal increase of almost 22 per cent on pre-war years. Given rising inflation, this was in real terms a reduction. The list of servants' names and positions remains the same as that provided in December 1917, except for the omission of three individuals: William Bancalari, Mrs Predell and Joseph Colborn. Presumably Mrs Predell had died in the intervening year as she was no longer receiving a pension; and it would appear that William Bancalari had left the College's employ, as his name vanishes from Servants' Committee minutes after December 1917. Meanwhile, it appears that Colborn's was just a temporary absence, as he is listed as being responsible for staircases 4, 5 and 9 in 1919,[69] following the restoration of peace and the return of undergraduates in residence.

These lists of names and wages suggest that, for the final years of the war, the College employed only about a dozen individuals to keep the College open and running – less than half of the 25 servants we know to have been employed in 1904.[70]

Just over a week after this meeting, the Armistice was declared and peace restored to the country; demobilisation meant a returning flood of students, Fellows and servants to Oxford. Detailed arrangements were required on staffing levels and pay. In contrast to the sporadic meetings of the Servants' Committee throughout the war, the committee met nine times throughout 1919, starting in March, when it was agreed that

> The wages of the Servants must be increased, that the authorised fees from Undergraduates should cease, that an increase in the Establishment Charges should therefore be made, that Women should be employed in College in addition to the Servants, that the Servants should have definite Staircases assigned to them and that each Servant should be assisted by a Woman, that the College Servants should be engaged by the month and paid monthly and subject to a month's notice. The Establishment Charges to be raised to in College Members to £7 a Term to out College Members to £3 a Term.[71]

The committee agreed on wages for the College porter, under porter, messenger, bootblack, scouts and women servants, and to employ a husband-and-wife team for the Common Room. It also decided to employ a pastry cook, which suggests that Balk either accepted the College's offer to be employed as its cook, or else had found work as a pastry cook elsewhere; a woman was preferred for his old post at Corpus, presumably so that the College could cut wages. The committee additionally wanted to employ a boy for the kitchen, deferring the appointment of a manciple until later: Knibbs was unwell and unable to fulfil his duties. In addition, staircases were assigned to individual servants; and the committee agreed upon the desirability of hiring a steward or stewardess to manage servants working in the kitchen.

The subsequent meeting in April tweaked some individual servants' staircase assignments and salaries, and Knibbs's illness was again alluded to in highlighting the need to make temporary arrangements for Trinity Term in the event of his continued absence. Meanwhile 'the question of Domestic Bursar [was] to be left to the College';[72] Henry Lightfoot's increased workload as Bursar was becoming unmanageable, a fact which is evident from the list of duties of the new Domestic Bursar drawn up at a subsequent College Meeting. The new appointment was to be responsible for 'ensuring the proper provisioning of the College', including the weighing and checking of meat, bread and other foodstuffs; keeping and checking 'all accounts, dinners, luncheons and breakfasts etc.'; keeping overall control of the College servants, subject to the Servants' Committee; keeping control of College 'staircases, rooms, furniture and valuations', including making periodic visitations of rooms during term; controlling and allocating 'coal and fuel, the Baths and heating apparatus'; ordering Buttery supplies and arranging prices; controlling the Senior Common Room and other rooms within Corpus; giving orders to the butler 'for all requirements such as crockery, linen, etc.'; superintending the 'cleaning of the Chapel and the Library', except for the books; making 'all necessary arrangements' for gaudies; and superintending the Annexe, subject to the government of the President.[73] At this same meeting Governing Body declared that 'both a male and female candidate should be considered' for the role; and although a Miss Brookes was interviewed, the job ultimately went to a man.[74] Howard Vincenté Knox, born in Trinidad in 1868, had studied Classics Moderations at Exeter College, Oxford, and had served in both the Boer War and First World War. He was appointed Bursar's Assistant in June 1919 (the post was renamed Domestic Bursar in 1923 after the Statute passed by the College came into effect), before leaving to become a research fellow in philosophy at Oxford's Manchester College two years later. He died in 1960, aged 91. Meanwhile, Henry Lightfoot, the College Bursar, remained in post until he died in November 1924 aged 74. He was succeeded by Lieutenant Colonel Aubrey Vere Spencer, who remained in post until 1946.[75]

Throughout summer 1919 the Servants' Committee met frequently to discuss individual servants' needs, salaries, pensions and contracts. The horrifying outbreak of the worldwide flu epidemic, however, was the sole subject of the meeting on 19 November, and the committee's recommendations were approved by Governing Body later that same day. Inoculation for the whole College, at the expense of Corpus, was scheduled for 22 November, and any undergraduate who failed to appear would be liable to be sent down. Servants, including women assistants, were also to be inoculated. In case of an outbreak, Lecture Room 3 was to be used as an isolation ward, with the bed from the Visitor's Room to be used for the first bed. In addition, a memorial service for Percival Woodcock (CCC 1919), who had died of malaria in College two days previously, was also arranged for 22 November; and the two St John's Brigade attendants who had attended him, Officer Greenaway and Mr Webb, were to be remunerated by the College – a duty which fell to the newly appointed Bursar's Assistant.[76] Woodcock's tragic death sent a shock wave through the College, and a £10 grant to cover his medical expenses was decreed by Governing Body in February 1920.[77] Knox was also to arrange with Greenaway, if possible, for 'an attendant to hold himself at the disposal of the College for night work, in the event of an epidemic of influenza'. If this was possible, Corpus would pay a donation 'to St John's Brigade in recognition of their allowing any such lieu on the services of any member'. It was also decided that the Vice President would try to make similar arrangements for a trained nurse.[78] The College made inquiries into all of this, and Governing Body were able to confirm Mr Greenaway's engagement as a night attendant at 12s. 6d. a night, and a donation of £3. 3s. 0d. was made to St John's Ambulance Brigade in consideration of their assistance. Meanwhile, a Mrs Maclachlan was retained as a nurse for Hilary Term at a weekly rate of £1. 1s. 0d. while not employed by Corpus, and £3. 13s. 6d. if needed and employed by the College.[79] The fact that no Corpuscle appears to have died of flu, therefore, seems to have reflected a combination of good luck and determined effort by Corpus staff.

4

CORPUS LIFE AND
BUILDINGS IN WARTIME

The University's War Effort

The war physically manifested itself all across Oxford during the course of 1914–18. The city was a military garrison, and at the city's heart the University featured heavily in local military roles. Young officers were trained in the cadet battalions formed in Oxford and quartered in the colleges. A School of Instruction for young officers was founded in December 1914; it opened in January 1915, and by March 1916 3,000 young men had passed through its doors. This school was superseded by two officer cadet battalions, each of about 750 individuals, and quartered in Balliol, Hertford, Keble, Magdalen, New, St John's, Trinity, Wadham and Worcester colleges. Also in 1915 the city saw the formation of a School of Military Aeronautics which after a short while changed into a cadet school and trained about 1,000 cadets. As we will see, several of these cadets and mechanics were housed at Corpus during the conflict; others lived at Brasenose, Christ Church, Exeter, Jesus, Lincoln, Pembroke and Queen's colleges. The school's aerodrome was located on Port Meadow; its camp in University Parks.

Meanwhile, the University's scientific laboratories were put at the disposal of the government for military purposes. Military success depends on scientific and technical efficiency and discovery; and wartime medicine and surgery were revolutionised during the conflict. Both these fields were helped enormously through work that was undertaken in Oxford University's science departments. As we have seen earlier, the University's Examination Schools were converted into the Third Southern General Hospital early on during the war, complete with a mortuary in the basement. In addition, Somerville College was emptied of its traditional academic occupants in order to become a branch hospital; subsequently a quadrangle at Oriel College housed the dispossessed Somerville students. University College became a further source of accommodation for hospital patients; and wartime nurses were quartered at Merton.[1] Thus every college had its own war stories and experiences; and this chapter explores everyday life and events within Corpus's walls during the years 1914–18.

Corpus Buildings

During the war Corpus found its buildings being used by several people and groups for a wide range of academic and military purposes. On 21 November 1914 Governing Body resolved 'that steps be taken to place the New Buildings [the Annexe built in 1884–5, now the Jackson Building] at the disposal of the Military Authorities, if they should desire it'.[2] The military authorities, it transpired, did wish to make use of Corpus. By early 1915 the New Buildings were occupied by officers of the 7th Battalion OBLI, 'thus making themselves,' declared editors of the *Pelican Record*, 'in their inanimate way, useful to the country'.[3] Such an offer had been made subject to conditions laid out in detail by President Case. College beds and furniture, as well as 'extras' normally required by residing undergraduates, would be provided free of charge; but any damage must be discharged by the military authorities. The military authorities would be charged for living and lighting. Similarly the College would not provide board, but the building's basement was made available 'for eating purposes'. Corpus was likewise unable to provide servants; and, given that the porter of the Annexe 'is now being supplied as a servant of the College his services will not be available'. The military authorities would therefore need to provide their own security for the building. No change in these negotiations could be made without Case's written permission.[4] J. Newton-King, commander of the 7th Battalion of the OBLI, wrote to Case two days later thanking him for placing the building at the disposal of his officers, and promising to ensure that his instructions were carried out.[5] Two officers were thereafter accommodated by the end of February, with the possibility of up to another eight joining them later.

It seems, however, that not every room in the Annexe was occupied by OBLI officers; at a meeting in February 1915 Governing Body made two further resolutions regarding the wartime use of College buildings for another purpose. In the event of the Annexe not being required by the War Office, the building was to be made available to the Belgian Refugee Committee until again being required by the College. Corpus was willing to provide board and lodgings during term time to 'not more than two Belgian Students, the conditions and rules to be settled by the Tutorial Body', with such permission being renewed termly.[6] Anticipating the potential arrival of Belgian refugee students within Corpus, Governing Body held a Special Meeting in March 1915, where the Report of the Committee on the Admission of Belgian Students outlined their conditions and rules of residence: 'that a Belgian Student should be admitted as a Commoner, and wear a gown in the College, should be charged nothing, and for board should have dinner in Hall free, except for other liquors but water, and should have an allowance to be fixed by the Bursar for breakfast and lunch.'[7] Trinity Term 1915 saw the arrival of one such undergraduate at Corpus, and the *Pelican*'s editors reflected the contemporary sympathy for Belgium and her people: 'regretting sincerely as we do the unhappy circumstances which attend his exile to Oxford, we are glad to welcome amongst us a representative of a nation so heroic as his has proved to be.'[8] Frustratingly, we know nothing about this individual, not even his name. After 1915 all references to Belgian students at Corpus disappear from College records: it seems that only one such individual ever arrived and he did not remain very long in College; and in time its buildings were required by others.

During the summer break in 1916 Corpus's Governing Body 'agreed to put 20 sets of rooms at the disposal of schoolmasters in retreat from September 11th to 14th'.[9] Shortly afterwards, autumn 1916 saw Corpus sharing the buildings with about 50 mechanics from the Royal Flying Corps, following enactment of the Defence of the Realm Act (1914). In August 1916 Major General F. F. Johnson CB wrote to the College ordering that 'possession shall be taken under the Defence of the Realm Act of all those buildings known as C.C.C. and situate at Oxford, in the Co. of Oxford, except such portions that are now or may hereafter be occupied by resident members of the said College.'[10]

These mechanics settled in Corpus's Front Quadrangle; while the few remaining undergraduates (numbering seven that Michaelmas Term) resided in the Gentlemen Commoners' Building, with the Fellows' Building reserved for academic purposes. Although the College retained use of the kitchen – Corpus's manciple sharing the space with a military chef – other College rooms were taken over in order to feed these military mouths. Lecture Room 3, opposite the Chapel door, became the sergeants' mess; and the ground floor room of the President's staircase served as their canteen.[11] Obviously the mechanics, unlike the OBLI who had resided in the Annexe, were not confined to the basement for their meals.

The corps' arrival also required some adjustment of the College's meal timetable. 'In consequence of the use of the Hall for meals by the Flying Corps School it was resolved to change the hours of Hall Dinner to 7.30pm on Sundays and Week Days',[12] although by spring 1917 the corps were apparently no longer eating in the Hall.[13] Adjustments to washing facilities were also needed while the corps were in residence. Two of the College bathrooms were designated for military use; but since this proved to be inadequate, 'the adage that cleanliness is next to godliness has found a somewhat literal expression in the installation of a military washing apparatus in the bicycle shed up against the wall of the Chapel'.[14] Thereafter, Royal Flying Corps cadets resided in Corpus during the Long Vacation of 1917, replacing the mechanics previously resident. Once more the juggling of mealtimes was required. Assistant Commander Major Aderley accepted President Case's proposals that on weekdays the College should dine in Hall at 7pm and the cadets at 7.45pm; while on Sundays the College should dine at 7.30pm and the cadets at 6.15pm, 'except that on Sundays and guest nights the dinner need not be in Hall if so desired by the majority of those dining: the time to be Greenwich time'.[15] Accommodating military personnel alongside Corpus's few remaining students evidently required ongoing logistical considerations.

Non-academics could be accommodated up to a point at Corpus; but, given its small size, there was a limit to how far the College could help the military. Thus in autumn 1917 Governing Body felt that they had to refuse requests from the War Office for quartering further military personnel at the College for three reasons. Firstly there were the difficulties of administration given the 'inadequacy of the College staff which has been much depleted in consequence of the war'. Secondly there were worries that the College would have 'no effective control over the cadets, or over the caterers, who would have to be employed by the College'. Thirdly there were the 'serious risks of loss which the College has not funds to meet'.[16] The continued residence of military figures within Corpus meant that further requests for other wartime requirements had to be refused again at the start of 1918:

> In answer to an inquiry by the Principal of St Edmund Hall as to whether the College would accept invalided and discharged officers as residents in connexion with schemes of the Ministry of Munitions by the Oxford Orthopaedic Centre, it was agreed that as so much of the College is already in military occupation, the College has at present only two sets of rooms available, which are unsuitable for invalids; it therefore regrets that it is not able to adopt the schemes suggested.[17]

However, at a General College Meeting held two days before the Armistice, the College also resolved that, with regard to a letter received from the Board of Agriculture, it desired to contribute towards the Small Holdings Colonies Acts of 1916 and 1918 'so far as it can safely do so, consistently with the future good of the College as owner of lands'. Before such a resolution could proceed, the President and Bursar were 'to ask Mr Justice Peterson, MA of the College [the Hon. Sir Alfred Frederick Peterson (CCC 1879–83, Hon.

Fellow 1920–2)], to recommend a real property lawyer to advise them on the Acts concerned and on the Circular Letter from the Board, with a view of the question whether, and how far, the College can safely proceed with the Resolution'.[18] College land was thus also put to military use outside Corpus walls, and in Botley Road the College was compelled in 1918 'to release grazing land west of Binsey Lane for allotments'.[19] After the declaration of peace a final resolution was made regarding military occupation, in which the President was to send to the War Office 'the agreement under which the War Office took over the College'; and 'to represent that the military should evacuate the College as soon as convenient', so that the College would have time to carry out any repairs needed in time for the return of its under-graduates from the war.[20] Thereafter the College's traditional purpose resumed and occupants returned in 1919.

Despite its numerous wartime visitors, Corpus buildings did continue to be used for a variety of traditional academic purposes throughout the conflict. The American art collector Edmund Perry Warren, a graduate of New College, was elected an Honorary Fellow of Corpus on 6 March 1915. As such he was allocated rooms at a Governing Body meeting in May: 'it was resolved to assign rooms to Mr E. P. Warren, Honorary Fellow, so long as they are not wanted for Fellows or under-graduates, at the normal rent.'[21] By Trinity 1915 he was residing in the Gentlemen Commoners' Building.

Throughout war and peace the College fabric continued to need attention. In November 1915 Governing Body resolved to appoint a committee 'to report on the question of installing electric lights in the Old Library and the Study Library';[22] its report was adopted three weeks later.[23] In February 1916 Governing Body made three further resolutions regarding the College fabric. Firstly, following the recent discovery that the Pelican Sundial was leaning 4½ inches towards the East, 'it was resolved to apply concrete to the base'. Meanwhile, the restoration and cleaning of the Rubens picture in the Chapel was deferred. Lastly, 'the question of clearing the damp in the lower Library was reported to the Library Committee'.[24] Thereafter, no decisions regarding College fabric were minuted during the war; either no other major problems presented themselves during the war years or else problems were ignored, unrecorded or fixed without comment.

Daily Life

Following the outbreak of war, Michaelmas Term 1914 brought an immediate reduction in the number of residents at Corpus, with only 26 undergraduate members in residence, nine of whom were freshmen. While College life was able to continue in much the same vein as before, nonetheless the emptiness of buildings was immediately felt, as the *Pelican Record* made clear:

> Life in Oxford has been altered rather in quality than in kind. Chapels, Halls, Lectures, Roll-calls continue as before, with only two differences: first, that khaki has become academic dress; and may be seen at lectures and even at lecterns, as well as in the streets; second, that everywhere numbers have been reduced. We are a reduced garrison that has suffered heavily and has been obliged to withdraw its outposts (New Buildings are empty, but for the *vir idoneus* who, according to statute, is still in command of them) and to call up any available reserves (a Senior Student and an Indian were matriculated in October). This Michaelmas term an attendance of 30 persons is accounted a well filled lecture; the singing in Chapel has a hard struggle to outmatch the organ; Junior Commoners' table in Hall has been completely evacuated, and at most other tables there are greater spaces of unoccupied tablecloth than of men.[25]

These 26 residing undergraduates dropped to 20 throughout the year as individuals continued to volunteer for military service; and by Michaelmas 1915 numbers were lower still, though the new academic year did welcome 11 freshmen to Corpus. Following the introduction of conscription in March 1916, numbers had fallen to 13 by Hilary Term, reduced again to a dozen in Trinity 1916, and to only seven by Michaelmas. In mid-1917 there were briefly only six junior members; but following the return of wounded Corpuscle Sir Edward Hale (CCC

1917–20) during the latter part of Trinity 1917, discharged from the front on medical grounds, undergraduate numbers returned to seven. Thereafter, there were only six students in residence in Michaelmas 1917. However, numbers crept up again to eight by summer 1918, including Charles Hignett (CCC 1915–16, 1918–22), who was well enough to return to Corpus after being invalided out from the Royal Garrison Artillery in 1917, and Charles Reginald Schiller Harris (CCC 1918–20), elected scholar from Clifton in 1914, who was demobilised before reaching the battlefields.[26] Undergraduate numbers had fallen again to seven by Michaelmas 1918; but the declaration of peace in November signalled the forthcoming return to more usual numbers, and by December 1918 the College had received word from 'a goodly number' who wished to return to Corpus. Editors of the *Pelican* wrote of the College's hopes that these men could be accommodated and that 'the War Office grants them the preferential treatment they deserve', in order to have them residing again in the new term.[27] Hilary 1919 saw the matriculation of 21 undergraduates at Corpus even though the Front Quad was 'still in the clutches of the War Office surveyors'.[28] Trinity 1919 saw 16 more come up, something that was made possible only because 'redecoration of those rooms which have led recently an unenviable existence as "billets" was finished in time for our return in April'.[29] Michaelmas 1919 brought another 24 undergraduates to the College.[30] With 55 junior members in residence six months after the restoration of peace, accommodating all Corpus's new and returning junior members proved something of a challenge. While a total of 61 Corpuscles were matriculated across three terms in 1919, thereafter undergraduate numbers returned to pre-war levels, with 24 freshmen beginning in 1920, and 20 freshmen arriving in 1921.

Meanwhile, rationing and widespread food shortages were increasingly felt as the war dragged on, making life for those who remained increasingly challenging and uncomfortable. Before the war Britain had relied on food imports for around 60 per cent of her food: wartime enemy targeting of merchant ships resulted in around 300,000 tonnes of Britain-bound shipping sunk every month; while a poor American harvest in 1916 made things worse. In December 1916 the Ministry of Food was established, headed by Lord Devonport, and later by Lord Rhondda, as Minister of Food Control. Its aim was to promote voluntary rationing; it urged citizens to restrict their consumption to a weekly maximum of 4lb of bread, 2½lb of meat and ½lb of sugar.[31] To this end Governing Body agreed early in 1917 that the manciple 'be permitted to provide a dinner exceeding 2/6 a head, but not exceeding 3/–, the difference to be charged to each person dining that day at High Table or Common table of the Fellows'.[32] Lord Devonport's orders were acted upon, and their effects were felt across Corpus. 'In consequence the College sparrows hold matutinal indignation meetings in the quad, before the College cat is afoot. Classical archaeologists are considering the propriety of resuscitating the singularly elegant Middle-Minoan fashion of wearing wasp-waist rings … At any rate fasting has now become as compulsory as praying.'[33] As food became increasingly expensive and more stringently rationed throughout the lean war years, mealtimes for those few remaining at Corpus must have felt progressively duller and sparser. Then in May 1917 the College resolved firstly 'that a census be taken of the wine in the College Cellar, under the instructions of the Bursar'; and secondly 'that expert opinion be called in to advise as to any measurements necessary for the preservation of the existing stock'.[34]

The end of 1917 saw further resolutions regarding food, as well as concerns about wartime damage. In December Governing Body agreed to renew anti-aircraft insurance for 1918.[35] Across Oxford, wartime Fellows 'worried about air raids and about whether to insure or remove their college's valuable property'. Such fears were reasonable, as London had suffered Zeppelin raids, and nearby Oxford 'was indeed an armed camp and therefore a legitimate military target'. The need to dim lights brought a 'general gloom' to Oxford, and Christ Church's Great Tom bell ceased to toll, leaving those who remained pining for the city's usual sights and sounds.[36] The blackout led to accidents across town. A soldier, Private Robert Harris, was killed by a bus in dark St Margaret's Road; and various precautions were taken across Oxford to meet safety concerns. In Cowley the bases of street lamps were painted white as a precautionary measure while, to the fury of some residents, 'fine trees in Banbury Road were felled in

December 1917 because people kept walking into them in the dark'.[37] At that same meeting in December 1917 Corpus Governing Body also agreed 'to have two non-meat dinners in Hall weekly on Wednesdays and Fridays until further notice'.[38] Thereafter, early 1918 heralded further decrees. In view of the rising food prices 'it was agreed to raise the maximum cost of High Table Dinner to 3/6, the cost above the dinner allowance to be charged to the persons dining'.[39] Further restrictions were introduced in spring 1918, when it was agreed that there should be a 'meatless guest night on Sundays'; that 'no teas be provided for undergraduates from the Kitchen at present'; and that 'no undergraduates be permitted to invite strangers except on meatless nights'.[40] Following the Armistice and the return to Corpus en masse of undergraduates, Fellows and staff, it was agreed at a College Meeting in January 1919 that, in order sufficiently to accommodate and feed everyone, during the term a 'common breakfast' would be provided in the Hall between 8.15am and 9.15am on weekdays (and between 8.30am and 9.30am on Sundays), 'after which time no breakfast will be served'. In addition a 'common lunch' would be provided between 1pm and 1.45pm on the same conditions. Those wishing to avail them-selves of this arrangement were requested to communicate with the Dean, and 'no one to change in the course of the term'. At the same meeting it was also agreed that 'dinner in Hall should be at 7pm on weekdays and 7.30 on Sundays for this term'.[41] Although the war was over, it took time to hail the end of rationing, and for the pre-war abundance and diversity of food to return.

Aside from rationing, heating the College was an additional problem in wartime. In February 1918 Governing Body resolved that, after hearing the report of the Library Committee, it 'accepted E. Herring's Report on improving the heating apparatus, which warms the Chapel, Library, Hall and Lecture Rooms III'; it stipulated that after full particulars had been obtained, 'the estimates and specifica-tions are submitted to the College for its approval'.[42] Three months later 'the Bursar was empowered to apply for a priority certificate from the Ministry of Munitions for a new heating apparatus, for the Hall and Library etc.'.[43] At a Meeting of Residents in October 1918 regarding coal supply 'the President was authorised to endeavour to obtain better terms for the College, and to report to the College'.[44] To residents' dismay, shortly after the Armistice, it was announced at a College meeting that

> the Coal Controller found that he could not separate the allowance
> of the College from that of the military, but would allow 215½
> tons altogether, to be shared by agreement, the College to accept
> responsibility for the exemption. An additional allowance for the
> baths to be agreed upon. The College accepted these terms.[45]

The declaration of the Armistice in November 1918 did not herald the end of fuel shortages. Editors of the December 1918 issue of the *Pelican Record* noted:

> This winter will not be an easy one for us, unless the Bursar can
> move the Coal Controller's stony heart. The Oxford way of life
> is not easily adapted to a fuel shortage, and half a ton of coal
> is a cruel allowance for undergraduates who are always invalids
> and usually invalided soldiers. Still, things might be worse: it has
> not yet been found necessary to burn the desks of Lecture Room
> No. 3.[46]

The war may have been over, but winter 1918 must nevertheless have felt harsh with inadequate heating during the cold, dark days and evenings, especially given that residents were on a diet of rationed food, and had few – if any – activities to distract them from the dreariness of the winter before the return of their friends from the front throughout 1919. The picture was the same across the whole of Oxford, as shortages of coal closed the city's restaurants and theatres earlier than usual. Those who stayed behind 'occasionally felt that each term in wartime had "an unbroken tenor of sad monotony"'.[47]

Aside from low undergraduate numbers and rationing and heating constraints, the occasional wartime rule or edict was made which had further impact on daily College life. In February 1915 Governing Body resolved to make it 'compulsory upon all undergraduate members of the College to attend at least one service in the Chapel on Sundays, unless they have conscientious objections: this rule to begin as from next term'.[48] This resolution was amended three months later, when 'it was resolved that attendance at evening Chapel on Sunday should count in lieu of an ordinary week-day roll-call'.[49]

The Great War also brought with it the introduction of British Summer Time to the UK, and at a meeting of Corpus Residents in May 1916, 'it was resolved in accordance with the Government's request to put forward the clock one hour as from 2am May 21st till September 30th inclusive'.[50] Meanwhile, the war disrupted some annual College events, but not all. No College gaudies were held between 1915 and 1918;[51] but it was agreed to continue the Pate School Governors' lunch in 1916.[52] Presumably, however, the Pate lunch was not held in 1917 or 1918, as it is not referred to during later wartime records. Doubtless wartime rationing would have made it hard to justify.

Academic Life

Although Corpus rooms were largely emptied of Fellows and under-graduates throughout the conflict, a degree of traditional academic study persevered, and several weekly lectures were still held in College. These included a series of lectures in logic provided by Schiller; while Grundy, during his sporadic periods of wartime residence within College, gave lectures on Rome and classical civilisations. When not occupied with work for the Ministry of Munitions, Jolliffe continued to provide weekly mathematics lectures at Corpus; Livingstone delivered a variety of Classics lectures; and, when he was away from the Naval Intelligence Department, Mowat provided weekly College lectures on English history. As the war progressed, the number of these weekly lectures fluctuated, but never ceased entirely. Occasionally additional lectures were provided within Corpus by external speakers: in Trinity 1915, Hilary 1916 and Hilary 1917 the Revd Mr Sherwood, the Mayor of Oxford, visited the College to lecture on Divinity.[53]

The Governing Body, in a meeting in December 1916, adopted a Tutorial Body Report concerning matriculations, recommending that during the course of the war 'there should be the usual examination for matriculations in April, and that after that the President should fill up vacancies as far as appears desirable with candidates who shall have passed Responsions'.[54] Responsions (usually nicknamed 'Little Go') was the examination that undergraduates were required to pass shortly after matriculating at the University: early 20th-century school exams were not standardised, so Responsions ensured that colleges were not accepting unqualified students. To pass the exams, undergraduates needed to answer relatively straightforward questions on Latin, ancient Greek and mathematics. Compulsory Greek was abolished from Reponsions in 1920; Latin was removed from the exam in the 1950s. During Governing Body meetings early in 1917, further decisions were made regarding scholarships in a reply sent to the Vice Chancellor. It was announced that the College 'agrees with the view that it is desirable to postpone any general reconsideration of College Scholarship examinations until the end of the war', and that the College was 'willing to renew the arrangement with Cambridge for 1917–8'.[55] This 'arrangement' with Cambridge involved the agreement of 'rotation' with groups of colleges within Oxford. Boys were to sit exams for available scholarships at several colleges within a particular group, rather than for an individual college. This (presumably) meant that scholarship awards could be pooled and shared out between the colleges, limiting how much funding each college needed to make available. That the same policy was implemented at Cambridge was agreed to be crucial to the success of rotation, and so the policy was renewed for another year. By October 1918 it became clear that the end of the war was in sight, and the Governing Body authorised the President 'to supply the War Office with a list of members of the tutorial staff of the College engaged in war work, with a view to a scheme for releasing them on the restoration of peace'.[56] The College was clearly keen to waste no time in confirming the return of its serving Fellows in order to resume teaching the pre-war levels of undergraduates anticipated to be in residence. Following the declaration of peace, a College meeting of February 1919 directed the President to 'invite applications from members of the College who desired to avail themselves of grants offered by the Board of Education', and to inquire of the Board of Education 'whether it will guarantee to the College

any disbursements made under this Scheme for Interim Grants'.[57]
Corpus, like the rest of the University, was keen to see ex-officers and
servicemen return to higher education, and desired that individuals'
inability to meet the expenses involved should not be a barrier to
doing so.

Student Clubs and Societies

The immediate reduction in undergraduate numbers at the outbreak
of war seriously reduced the range and scope of extracurricular activities in Michaelmas 1914:

> Thus the only recreation that has survived is rowing, and the
> freshmen are being subjected to the usual ordeal of 'tubbing'. We
> believe that the senior undergraduates seek health and diversion in
> table tennis. No College society meets except the Sundial, which
> has held three successful meetings. But, of course, all is subordi-
> nated to the work of the Officers' Training Corps, which in these
> troubled days absorb much time.[58]

By Hilary 1915 the number of undergraduates residing in Corpus had
dropped to 22, bringing about the complete cessation of any student
sports clubs functioning within College, although the Sundial Society
was still able to hold regular meetings.[59] The OTC was the only extracurricular activity continuing to run successfully. By Trinity 1915 there
were two fewer undergraduates within Corpus walls. Editors of the
Pelican Record regaled with humour the resulting lack of extracurricular activities, and the lengths to which residing students would go
to produce some entertainment:

> In the present depressing circumstances our best thanks are due to
> those gentlemen who are using their talents to enliven the College.
> It is no doubt to this charitable intention that we are to attribute
> the epidemic of pianos which has set in this Term. One staircase
> can boast of no less than three of these fascinating instruments;
> and we have it on good authority that the owner of one of them

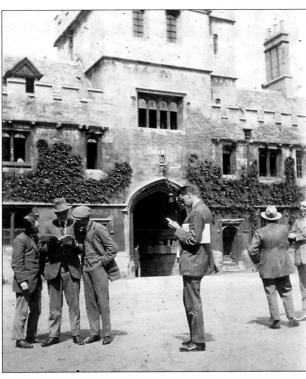

1. Corpus Christi College Front Quad, c.1911.

2. Corpus 23rd President, Thomas Case (CCC President 1904–24), 1913.

3. Corpus Christi College Boat Club VIII, 1909.
Back row: C. A. Gladstone (Christ Church), J. D. Mackworth, R. W. Dugdale (KIA 23 Oct 1918) and C. R. Haigh (KIA 7 Nov 1914); *Middle row*: L. F. Nalder, G. O. W. Willink (KIA 28 Mar 1918), S. Vaux, C. Bushell, VC (KIA 8 Aug 1918) and E. E. Potter; *Front row*: L. Powell.

4. Corpus Christi College Pelican Essay Club, 1910.
Back row: P. M. Baker, D. W. A. Hankey (KIA 12 Oct 1916), E. F. W. Baelz, L. F. Nalder, P. J. Patrick, A. H. Simpson, R. W. Dugdale (KIA 23 Oct 1918) and T. H. W. Barker; *Second row*: R. B. Mowat (CCC Fellow), W. J. T. P. Pythian-Adams, A. Sidgwick (CCC Fellow), E. M. H. Lloyd, E. L. Woodward, Revd. C. Plummer (CCC Fellow and Chaplain) and F. C. S. Schiller (CCC Fellow); *Front row*: W. M. Ogle, H. S. Smith (KIA 18 Aug 1916), R. H. Crump, L. Powell and R. I. Bottomley.

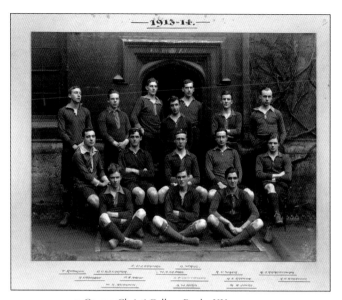

5. Corpus Christi College Rugby XV, 1913–14.
Back row: E. St J. Bamford and D. Veale; *Third row*: T. Robinson (KIA 25 Oct 1918), E. C. D. S. Carter, W. H. D. de Pass (KIA 25 Mar 1918), R. C. Wace and G. B. Ramsbotham (KIA 16 May 1915); *Second row*: A. Chavasse (KIA 5 Jul 1917), F. B. Geidt, H. F. Chittenden, H. L. Rayner (KIA 1 Jul 1916) and R. O. Hobhouse; *Front row*: W. A. D. Goodwin (KIA 1 Jul 1916), D. W. Hurd (KIA 15 Sep 1916) and M. H. Jones.

6. RAF cadets at Corpus Christi College, May 1918.

ARTURO ELAM HAIGH A·M·
HVIVS COLLEGII PER XXXI ANNOS
DISCIPVLO PRAELECTORI SOCIO
HOC MARMOR POSVERE
COLLEGAE ET AMICI·

VIR SANVS IVDICIO, CONSILIO PRVDENS, LABORE INDEFESSVS
COLLEGIVM ET ACADEMIAM
STVDIIS ET LITTERARVM CVLTV ORNAVIT
DE GRAECORVM THEATRIS ATTICAE TRAGOEDIAE POETIS
ERVDITISSIME DISSERVIT
DOCTRINAE PORTAS MVLTIS APERVIT
DISCENTIBVS OPEM FERRE NVNQVAM NON PARATVS
MORBO EX IMPROVISO INGRAVESCENTE
DIE XX° DECEMBRIS MCMV
LIBERIS ET AMICIS MVLTVM DEFLENDVS OCCVBVIT
ANNOS L NATVS

EIVSDEM FILIVS MAIOR NATV CAROLVS RODERICVS HAIGH A·B HVIVS COLLEGII
IVVENIS VITÆ INTEGERRIMÆ PIETATE ERGA DEVM ET NECESSARIOS INSIGNI
MILES ACER PRO PATRIA DIMICANS IN FLANDRIA CECIDIT
IDEM TESTAMENTO AMOREM ET PATRIS ET COLLEGII PROBAVIT
ERGO GRATES NOSTRAS INSCRIPSIMVS IN PATRIS MONVMENTO
OBIIT VII° DIE MENSIS NOVEMBRIS
ANNO DOMINI MCMXIV
ÆTATIS SVÆ XXVII

7. The Haigh memorial, Corpus Cloisters. Charles Roderick Haigh (CCC 1907–10) was killed during the First World War, aged 26; this memorial was appended to that of his father, Arthur Elam Haigh (CCC Fellow 1901–5).

8. Henry George Ward (CCC Servant appointed 1912) was killed in action on 23 July 1916. He was Corpus's youngest wartime casualty, aged just 17.

Pte. H. G. WARD, Old Marston, Oxf. and Bucks Lt. Infy.—Wounded and missing.

9. Alfred William Clifford (CCC Servant) was killed in action on 25 September 1915, aged 21.

Pte. A. W. CLIFFORD, Alexandra-road, 5th O.B.L.I.—Missing.

Ranna P.O.
Bengal
22.v/15
The President of
Corpus Christi College
Oxford

Dear Sir,

You will, before this letter reaches you, have heard of my brother Geoffrey Ramsbotham's death in action on Sunday, May 16th. I think he must have fallen in the storming of the German lines at Festubert. I take the liberty of writing to tell you how dearly he loved his College, and of the affectionate respect that he had for yourself, sir, personally. I hope, when I get my leave, that I may be able to come & see his rooms in the College which he loved so well.

I think that Geoffrey, like many Corpus men, had a very high sense of duty, and that the College emblem of the Pelican plucking its heart was of very real significance to him. Well he gave his lifeblood for England, and he died like an English gentleman.

I'm so proud to think he was a scholar of C.C.C. Forgive my trespassing on your time — but I thought you would like to know that Geoffrey was very proud to be on the foundation of your College.

Ever very truly

R. B. Ramsbotham

10. Letter to President Thomas Case from R. B. Ramsbotham, 22 May 1915, regarding the death of his brother, Geoffrey Bury Ramsbotham.

11. The Corpus First World War memorial. Located next to the
altar in the College Chapel, it was erected 1921–2.

12. Corpus Christi College Front Quad, photographed in 2018.

will soon be able to play easy tunes with one hand almost without mistake. Such is the reward of patience and self-sacrifice.[60]

Despite low numbers the Sundial Society was able to maintain its busy schedule of meetings in 1915, and the College Lawn Tennis Club was thanked for organising a Singles Handicap and, 'what is perhaps even more important, for the provision of tea at the ground'.[61] The introduction of 11 new freshmen after the Long Vacation of 1915 briefly regalvanised the Boat Club throughout Michaelmas and Hilary terms; and tennis and punting were again available throughout Trinity 1916. However, undergraduate numbers continued to fall steadily, and editors of the *Pelican*'s June 1916 issue warned that 'the prospect of a winter term with Oxford weather is too appalling to think of'.[62] The Sundial Society, the final activity to succumb to the depletion of numbers in College, ceased to meet in summer 1916, but revived in Michaelmas Term and continued to meet throughout 1917. None of the sports clubs was able to re-form after summer 1916, however, as undergraduate numbers were down to single figures.[63] Meanwhile, as the war continued, editions of the *Pelican Record* became ever more slender as fewer members of Corpus were in residence to contribute to its pages, and as paper became scarcer and more expensive. By the end of 1917 editors apologised:

> In view of the dearth of paper and of news it is contemplating a self-denying ordinance and a reduction in the number of its appearances. It may, therefore, prove expedient to postpone the publication of the next Number until June, 1918, unless the situation should be radically changed before then by the conclusion of a Victorious Peace, when of course it would become the P.R.'s manifest duty to mobilize the noble army of Corpus poets, and to celebrate our Fourth Centenary by a Special Number.[64]

The June 1918 issue of the *Pelican* confirmed this motion, apologising that 'the dearth and high price of paper compel us to appear but twice yearly'.[65] Though peace was declared in November, paper continued to remain expensive, so the College magazine remained twice yearly until

1920. With over 50 undergraduates back in residence by mid-1919, however, student clubs and societies were quick to re-form following the restoration of peace: the Boat Club, Pelican Essay Club, Sundial Society, Wasps, Rugby, Athletics and Lawn Tennis were able to meet early in 1919, and the Owlets did so from Michaelmas.

400th Anniversary

From the early stages of the war the College's Governing Body had anticipated that the conflict would put paid to any quatercentenary celebrations. At a meeting in February 1915 'it was resolved that the College will not celebrate the fourth centenary of its foundation before 1917'.[66] Faint hopes that the war would be over in time for the celebrations to take place on schedule were evidently still alive in autumn 1916, but were rapidly diminishing: 'It was resolved that if possible the Fourth Centenary of the College be celebrated in the College in 1917, if the War is over, and if not, as soon as possible after the conclusion of the War.'[67] At the end of 1916 the College asked itself 'in these troublous times how will it be possible to rejoice with a whole heart, and to gather together all those who would be delighted to do honour to the memory of Richard Foxe?' Although celebrating the 400th anniversary of Claymond's possession of the College on 5 March 1517 became impossible, some hope remained that 'it may be found possible to celebrate 15 September 1517, when he was "admitted"'.[68]

The year 1917 arrived, and the war continued to rage. In May 1917 the College agreed to defer the question of any quatercentenary celebrations until October;[69] and at the end of the year it was deferred again until summer 1918.[70] Thus the 400th anniversary of the College's foundation passed without any major celebrations. It is clear, however, that Corpus marked the occasion in some way, although without the pomp and circumstance originally hoped for. A letter now in the College Archives from the former bishop of Winchester, the Rt Revd Edward Talbot (CCC Visitor 1911–23), written in 1929 to the Corpuscle and Poet Laureate Robert Bridges (CCC 1863–7, Honorary Fellow 1895–1930), sheds some light on the Chapel service held to mark the occasion:

I think our last effective meeting was at that queerly managed 400th celebration at C.C.C., when, as you said, we had so much of the Old Testament. That was extraordinarily unintelligent; but, as you will understand, in my view it was worse to have kept the anniversary of the College of that Name without so much as any Celebration of the Sacrament! Extraordinarily gauche to say no more. So also it was, when there were hardly any speakers, to call upon *two* Bishops.[71]

With so many members away at the front, Corpus Chapel apparently saw a very high clergy-to-congregation ratio on that occasion; and it is evident that Talbot, at least, was also somewhat unimpressed with other aspects of the service.

Following the restoration of peace in November 1918, there are no accounts of celebrations within College records marking the war's end. Presumably, as was the case at Trinity, this was because 'there was no college community to hold them'.[72] Corpus did, however, hold two College gaudies as part of ongoing celebrations in 1920: one for senior College members and alumni; and another for those members who had been on military service. The 1919 gaudy, planned for September, had to be cancelled due to the ongoing nationwide railway strike; the gaudy's organisers insisted that '"cancelled" is perhaps hardly the word; rather it is a deferred pleasure'.[73] Presumably this disappointment of 1919 fuelled determination to ensure that the College celebrated properly in 1920; after all, no gaudy had been held for six years. While invitations to such gaudies were usually sent only to Corpuscles who kept their names on the books, 'in this instance it is proposed, as far as accommodation allows, to send invitations to others also, in the case of those who have been on military service',[74] in order to allow for as many former soldiers as possible to take part in the celebrations. The War Service Dinner was held on 20 April 1920, a date which was agreed to be preferable to an evening during the Long Vacation or immediately before the start of Michaelmas Term: 'the time of year is unusual, but Oxford needs not June for beauty's heightening, and the date will suit schoolmasters, who are otherwise occupied in October'.[75] There were 44 guests present at this dinner, with 56 members in total. Members dined on starters including Tortue Claire, Darnes de Saumon à Lucullus, and Œufs de Pluvier en aspic; a main course of Poulet à l'Anglaise, Quartier d'Agneau, Cœur de Laîtues aux Fines Herbes, Haricots Verts and Pommes de Terre Nouvelles; and a pudding of Pêche Melba, with accompanying dessert wine.[76]

For the 1920 gaudy held on 5 October 1920, 63 invitations were accepted, with a total of 73 College members present. Since special 400th anniversary celebrations never materialised, the 1920 College gaudy stood in the place of the missed anniversary. Named 'Fourth Centenary Dinner in Commemoration of the Founder', the celebratory menu consisted of Hors d'Œuvres Variés, Tortue Claire, Filets de Soles à la Cardinal, Bouchées à la Toulouse and Selle de Mouton to start; Filet de Bœuf, Chouxfleurs Béchamel, Pommes Duchesse, Perdreaux and Salade à l'Anglaise for the mains; with Pêche Melba for dessert, accompanied by coffee and dessert wine.[77] The gaudy was deemed a success, and editors of the *Pelican Record*'s December 1920 issue gushed: 'The long-deferred Fourth Centenary of the foundation of the College', impossible to hold in war-torn 1917 and deferred in 1919 following the national railway strike, 'proved to be a case not so much of "better late than never", as of "better than could have been believed"'. The College had 'fortified itself for the occasion by selecting five from the long list of distinguished Corpuscles and adding them to itself as Honorary Fellows, and all of these duly attended'. The Bishop of Winchester, the College Visitor, had also been invited; and despite him being the visitor of 'no less than five Oxford Colleges', he duly came and 'did not disdain to read the second lesson in the Commemoration Service'. As a result, the *Pelican*'s editors noted, 'there were plenty of bishops and of good cheer, of good speeches (by the bishops), and of good cheer (by the audience) to gratify the *manes* of the Pious Founder! ... Suffice it to say that the Commemoration Dinner proved quite as successful as the War Gaudy in the Easter Vacation.'[78] Evidently the restoration of peace and a seeming return to pre-war life at Corpus, coupled with a delayed marking of the College's 400th anniversary, produced a successful celebration.

CORPUS AFTER THE ARMISTICE

Following the Armistice on 11 November 1918 and the restoration of peace, Corpus, like the rest of Oxford, seemed to return to its pre-war normality at remarkable speed. After Corpus had been almost emptied of undergraduates for four years, 1919 saw the matriculation of 61 undergraduates across three terms, roughly three times the number who had matriculated annually at Corpus in the pre-war years. The Hilary and Trinity terms of 1920 each saw another undergraduate matriculate; but thereafter, from Michaelmas 1920, when 22 young men came up, numbers of freshmen returned to pre-war levels. With its Fellows and undergraduates restored, Oxford academic life, its sports and extracurricular activities, could return to peacetime normality. Frank Donnison (CCC 1919–21) matriculated in Trinity Term 1919 and recounted his idyllic experiences of post-war Corpus in contrast to the horrors he had experienced at the front:

> In the space of a few months we had experienced the extremes of human life, from the trenches to this heaven-sent summer term in Oxford. I remember very well lying alone in a punt in the New Cut of the Cherwell, the sky a golden sunset glow, the water still and luminous with fading light, the line of poplars tall and black against the sky, and feeling a deep thankfulness flow through me: that I was alive, that I was in this meltingly lovely place, above all that life held a future again.[1]

Nonetheless, the aftermath of the war had long-lasting and life-changing consequences across Oxford University, including some curriculum changes and the increasing acceptance of women. Juxtaposed against such changes, however, were many people across the whole of the country who seemed determined to try to forget the horrors of war as best they could: a wish to restore normality was widespread. Once the war was over, Vera Brittain noted, 'almost immediately, Oxford became abnormally normal.'[2] Corpus, like Oxford, was no exception.

The scarcity of relevant College records in the aftermath of the First World War makes it impossible for us to know how returning war veterans related to other junior members, and how easy such Corpuscles found it to 'fit in' alongside those who had been too young to face the horrors of the battlefields. Such relationships seem to have been amicable enough in Oxford generally. Certainly at neighbouring Christ Church the Modern History tutor John Masterman 'remembered both the "speed and determination with which Oxford resumed its peacetime life" and the "wide and healthy tolerance of the returning warriors which enabled them to continue and coalesce easily and amicably with the younger men"'. Furthermore, Curthoys notes that 'the influence of the older men was good, and they tolerated rules which must have seemed childish with remarkable patience and good humour. The college had probably never been so mixed, so democratic or so full.'[3] Meanwhile Grundy later remembered those who came up to Corpus after the restoration of peace as

> one of the most satisfactory generations in the college that I experienced in my thirty-odd years as tutor ... the most remarkable characteristic of them was their keenness to resume the studies on which they had been engaged before being called away. Several of them took first-classes in the Final Classical School and one of them got the best first-class of his year.[4]

Corpus, like Oxford and the rest of the country, could not of course recover its lost pre-war world. The restoration of normality was no more than skin-deep and the lost friends, colleagues and loved ones could not be forgotten. 'The University and colleges were soon restored to their pre-war appearance, but conditions were different. Harold Macmillan could not bear to return and finish his degree: "I just could not face it. To me it was a city of ghosts."'[5] Up and down the country, the need to remember and honour those who had died became manifest in the construction of war memorials; and this was as true at Corpus as anywhere else. Corpus began making plans to erect a war memorial to honour its war dead within a matter of months after the signing of the Armistice; but it was several years before the memorial was created, because of debate about exactly what form the memorial should take, and where in College it should be. In March 1919 Corpus Governing Body passed the following initial motion about its construction: 'War Memorial: It was agreed that the architectural memorial should consist of a slab with a list of names, placed in a conspicuous position in the College. Further schemes were postponed with a view to allowing suggestions to be sent in to the President.'[6] Two months later, Governing Body mooted the idea of putting a memorial tablet at the east end of the Cloisters where, after all, other College memorials were already located; and a committee of the President, Grundy and Livingstone was formed to decide on the war memorial's construction. One question this committee needed to resolve was whether the memorial should 'draw a distinction between actual and potential members of the College'.[7]

Next door at Christ Church, a war memorial book and tablets (recording names and honours, without military ranks) were paid for by the College. Christ Church's ambitious plans to fund new accommodation went out to an unsuccessful appeal; however, the funds raised, 'insufficient for any building scheme to get off the ground', eventually paid for the memorial garden.[8] Meanwhile, Oriel erected its war memorial on the wall of the Old Buttery, and 'a fund was opened for scholarships and exhibitions to be devoted in the first instance to the sons of those who had fallen in the war'.[9] At Corpus it was quickly agreed that the College would meet the bill for constructing the war memorial, rather than rely on an appeal to old members; but the committee had difficulty in deciding where to put it, or indeed in reaching any decisions on its appearance and contents. In the June 1919 issue of the *Pelican Record*, its editors explained that the Governing Body has decided to make no appeal, but to erect a memorial tablet to the fallen at the expense of the College. And, though we have a Quatercentenary to celebrate, a victory to commemorate, and a long list of heroes to bespeak the gratitude of coming generations, their decision perhaps deserves a word of commendation. The door is not barred to any individuals who may wish to offer individual subscriptions to other needy objects, as the note on College Clubs in this issue indicates. The position of the Memorial Tablet has been debated; alternative sites suggested were the College porch, opposite the porter's lodge, and the east wall of the cloisters, close to the Senior Common Room. The former was recommended, as bringing the memory of the dead more visibly and constantly before the eyes of their successors; the latter, by the association with our other memorial tablets. No inscription has been settled upon nor have any further steps been taken in the matter, and suggestions of any kind from old members of the College will be heartily welcomed.[10]

It was almost another year, however, before decisions were made or further action was undertaken.

Corpus looked at other Oxford college war memorials for its inspiration: early in June 1920 President Case received a letter from the literary scholar William Paton Ker at All Souls College, listing the sculptor (presumably of their own memorial) as J. M. H. Furse of Halsdon, Dolton, Devon, 'brother of the Bishop and of Charles Furse the painter who died some years ago'.[11] Furse was considered for appointment as the sculptor of the Corpus memorial, though its creation and installation were, at this stage, still several years away. About a fortnight later the committee reported that at its first meeting it had 'favoured the employment of white marble ... the names to be cut and coloured'. The committee then visited Hertford College to view its war memorial and decided that 'They liked it on the whole, but did not like the bronze used for the inscription, especially as bronze tends to lighten in the open air, and thought that the panels ought to be wooden, and the central panel also for the inscription'. They were given an estimated cost of £800 for such a memorial in marble, or £600 for one in Portland stone. A third meeting of the committee, which revealed the costs of stone memorials at Magdalen and Christ Church as each being roughly £500, helps to clarify why they favoured a memorial of wooden panels: 'It was concluded that these figures meant a serious expense to the College, especially in its present financial condition. It was suggested that an alternative in wood should be considered by the College.'[12] It is unclear from the College records who suggested the idea of putting the war memorial in the Chapel; but it appears that Grundy was critical of the scheme, at least initially: 'in the first place the chapel demands restoration, and no permanent work should, I think, be put in it until that restoration is done. In the second place the memorial should not, I think, be hidden away from sight, but be placed in such a position that everyone may see it.'[13] Perhaps Grundy was thinking of neighbouring Christ Church; nobody who enters the cathedral could fail to notice its extraordinary memorial tablets. By contrast, Corpus's war memorial is almost hidden from sight next to the Chapel altar. However, it seems that Grundy's concerns about the unsuitability of the Chapel were not shared by others at Corpus, for at a meeting of the Governing Body two days later, it was decided that the names to appear on the memorial should 'be inscribed on wooden tablets', and that they would be placed 'in the woodwork on the North side of the Chapel near the altar' – although at this stage the College was keen to have a memorial inscription 'on a brass plate on the East wall of the Chapel adjoining the names'; and the President was requested to consult with the Poet Laureate Robert Bridges (CCC 1863–7, Honorary Fellow 1895–1930) about ideas for an inscription in English and about the lettering.[14] However, the Poet Laureate was evidently not enamoured with the idea of composing an inscription for the College war memorial: in August 1920 R. W. Livingstone wrote to President Case: 'I am sorry that Bridges has thrown the whole thing up, because I think that we ought to have a really memorable inscription and I believe that he could have written one.'[15] Thereafter, an inscription by Charles Plummer, the College Chaplain, was chosen and settled upon at a meeting on 6 November 1920, almost exactly two years after peace was declared:

AD MAIOREM DEI GLORIAM
POSTERIS IN EXEMPLVM
ET IN PIAM ET PERPETVAM MEMORIAM
HIC IVXTA DEI ALTARE
HVIVSCE COLLEGII ALVMNORVM
NOMINA ADSCRIPSIMVS
QVI IN BELLO PER QVATTVOR ANNOS GESTO
MCMXIV–MCMXVIII
PRO REGE ET PATRIA
PRO FIDE ET IUSTITIA
VITAM POSVERVNT
AVETE FORTES ANIMAE
BENE VALEATIS IN PACE

In English, this reads:

To the greater glory of God
As an example to those who come after
And in pious and eternal memory,
Here, next to the altar of God,
We have written the names
Of the alumni of this College
Who, in a war waged over the four years
1914–18
Laid down their lives
For King and country
For faith and justice:
Greetings, mighty souls,
May you prosper in peace.[16]

On 11 January 1921 the President had an interview in Corpus Chapel with Mr Evans of Syme and Co., and Mr Barnes, Senior Partner of the firm Messrs Farmer and Bindley. Mr Evans agreed to do the carpentry for the war memorial, with Mr Barnes undertaking the lettering. In the report of the committee ten days later it was agreed that a brass plaque would not be required for the inscription because there was room on three oak panels 'not only for all the names of the fallen and their regiments, but also for the Inscription on the higher part of the middle panel'. Like the war memorial in Hertford College Chapel, names were to be in block capitals, and all the letters would be inscribed and gilded.[17] Between April and July 1921 correspondence flew back and forth between President Case and H. W. Barnes, regarding the drawing and setting out of lettering for the three panels; at the end of July arrangements were made to gild the names and silver the inscription, and it was estimated that 'the whole of the memorial shall be fixed complete not later than the end of September'.[18] The exact date of the memorial's erection in the Chapel is not recorded; but by December 1921 editors of the *Pelican Record* could report its completion; and a photograph of the memorial in situ appeared at the front of the March 1922 issue. Names of the fallen fill three panels: undergraduates and undergraduates-elect are listed by date of death, which, with regiments and ranks, follow the names; and the names of the two servants who fell appear at the end. The inscription, in silver lettering, occupies the upper part of the central panel. The layout of Corpus's war memorial thus differs from those of several other colleges. Merton's war memorial lists the names of the fallen without ranks;[19] at Magdalen, names are listed alphabetically without reference to military rank, and include college servants alongside old members, even Jacobs, the college's jobbing bricklayer.[20]

An additional 'alternative' wartime memorial, however, was rejected by members of Corpus, due to its rather unusual and somewhat unsuitable nature. Early in 1920 the College had received a letter from the War Office offering a 'heavy German gun and carriage'. At the College Meeting held on St Valentine's Day, Governing Body declared in the minutes that 'while appreciating the honour done to it by the offer, [it] regrets that it is unable to find any space to accommodate the gun'.[21] Editors of the *Pelican Record* were more forthright in their sense of bewilderment at the offering:

> It is prudent to fear the War Office, even when it is bearing gifts.
> If the matter of the Trojan Horse had been left to the young
> men, instead of being bungled by their elders (who were far too

much infatuated with Argive Helen to think of trying their 'war criminals'), they would no doubt have made an excellent bonfire of it, and Troy might be standing still. But even they could hardly have made light of 'a German heavy gun and carriage' (not said to be *paid*!), which was recently offered to the safe keeping of the College by the competent military authority. So it is doubtful whether they would have found a more judicious answer than the polite formula which has so often protected the College from a nuisance, viz. that 'owing to its small size' it really had no accommodation for it. It is regrettable, no doubt, that no more manageable memento of the Great War was offered us, and that so the College should have been driven into exhibiting apparent disrespect towards any Big Gun. But who could have contemplated the impiety of displacing the Pelican in the front quad, or the fatuity of obstructing the President's Drive, and leaving our trophy an easy prey to nocturnal raids of jealous neighbours? The cricket ground was considered as a possible site, but the responsible authority feared that it would act as a magnet and attract hordes of juvenile trespassers in vacation.[22]

Corpus records do not disclose what, if anything, eventually became of this proffered trophy.

Although he had apparently not felt able to devise an inscription for Corpus's war memorial, Robert Bridges was nonetheless the author of a different tract in the war's aftermath which, though not affecting the College directly, seems worth mentioning here. After the Treaty of Versailles was signed in 1919, Bridges, fearful of the Treaty's long-term effects, was a vocal advocate of the League of Nations. In the following year he initiated what is known as the Oxford Letter to the German Professors, an enterprise that affirmed a willingness by the signatories to resume communication with German academics who had been blamed for misleading the people in the war. The letter was printed in *The Times* newspaper in October 1920 and caused a considerable stir. The response to Bridges's initiative was largely hostile. Many Oxford academics refused to sign it, and were keen to distance themselves from the letter's sentiments; still others declared that because it was not signed by the University Chancellor it reflected the feelings of individuals, rather than Oxford academics at large. According to a note sent to Bridges from the classical scholar Cyril Bailey, Corpus's R. W. Livingstone was one of those who refused to sign Bridges's letter; and, similarly, 'no one else in CCC will sign, so I suppose this includes the President'.[23] Nevertheless, Bridges's Oxford Letter did generate numerous positive replies from across both the German- and English-speaking worlds. Walter Horn, director of the Deutsches Entomologisches Museum, told Bridges in November 1920 that he had 'done here always my best, from the beginning of this desolate war, to work in the same sense of reconciliation'; and told Bridges that the museum's motto, 'All men of science are brothers', was created in 1915.[24] Similarly, the teacher and historian Oscar Browning said later in October 1920 that 'for the first time in my life I wished to be an Oxford man'; and that if there was ever to be a Cambridge equivalent, 'I should much like to add my name to some similar statement'.[25]

Besides commissioning the war memorial itself, Corpus received a number of bequests from several fallen Corpuscles, or their families. These were to assist with various aspects of College life at the same time as remembering the individuals who did not return from the battlefields. The first of these, the Haigh Bequest, initially emerged in 1915, but could be acted upon only five years later, following the restoration of peace. Further bequests included the Radcliffe Boat Club fund, set up in 1920; the Maude College Barge, opened in 1930; the Christopher Bushell Prize, established in 1923; the Ramsbotham Silver Cup, donated in 1915; and the de Pass donation of books and funds for purchasing further books for the Library, given in 1919.

The minutes of the General College Meeting on 13 February 1915 are accompanied by an unnamed newspaper cutting from 6 June 1916 under the title 'Fallen Officer's Scholarship for Oxford', regarding the will of (Charles) Roderick Haigh (CCC 1907–10). Haigh, a professional soldier since 1911, was the son of the late Arthur Elam Haigh (CCC Fellow 1901–5) and, following Roderick's death in action at Ypres Salient on 7 November 1914, left, amongst other bequests elsewhere, '£2,300 to the President and Fellows for the time being of Corpus Christi College, Oxford, to found a scholarship or annual prize in memory of Arthur Elam Haigh, or to be used for any other purpose in memory of the said Arthur Elam Haigh, as the President and Fellows for the time being of the said college determine'. At the meeting the Governing Body desired 'to place on record its great regret at his death, and its sense of the generosity of the terms of his will', and established a committee, consisting of Plummer, Schiller, Livingstone and Clark, to consider the best means of carrying out the terms of Haigh's bequest.[26] At a College Meeting 15 months later, the investment of the balance of the bequest was approved, and it was agreed that the bequest would provide an annual Classics exhibition of £50 'to be filled up by competition among members of the College who have not exceeded sixteen terms of academical studying after one examination in classics'.[27] Meanwhile, during late 1915 or early 1916, an additional inscription was added to A. E. Haigh's memorial tablet on the north wall of the Cloisters, as a memorial to his son:

> Eiusdem filius maior natu Carolus Rodericus Haigh A.B. huius Collegii Iuvenis vitae integerrimae pietate erga Deum et necessarios insigni Miles acer pro patria dimicans in Flandria cecidit Idem testamento amorem et patris et Collegii probavit Ergo grates nostras inscripsimus in patris monumento. Obit vii° die mensis Novembris Anno Domini MCMXIV Aetatis suae XXVII.[28]

Translated, this reads:

> His elder son Charles Roderick Haigh, BA of this College, a young man of the purest life, of outstanding piety towards God and his friends, died as a bold soldier fighting for his country in Flanders. He in his will proved his love for his father and his College. Accordingly we have inserted our thanks on his father's monument. He died on 7 November in the year of our Lord 1914 in the 27th year of his age.[29]

The Roderick Haigh Exhibition came into force in 1920,[30] and two book prizes for Classics Moderations were also established from the bequest in 1922.[31] The Haigh Prize continues to this day, awarded to the Classics undergraduate who ranks first out of all the Corpus students in Finals.[32]

In 1920 Corpus was delighted to receive a trust fund for the Boat Club in honour of David Radcliffe (CCC 1913–14), following his death in action near Loos on 18 March 1916. A letter from Radcliffe's father was read aloud at a College Meeting in February, and Governing Body resolved that 'The College unanimously approves the acceptance of a trust fund to be established by Mr F. M. Radcliffe in memory of his late son David Radcliffe, and heartily approves the object of the proposed trust, and thanks Mr Radcliffe for his generous offer and the great interest he thereby shows in the welfare of the College'.[33] The next issue of the *Pelican Record*, appearing in March, recorded the benefaction. During his year as an undergraduate at Corpus, Radcliffe had rowed position 'two' in the Eights of 1914. He had enlisted after the outbreak of war in 1914, and had served in France with the Royal Fusiliers until his death in March 1916. In his son's memory, Mr Radcliffe offered Corpus £500 invested in the War Loan, with two years' accrued interest, held as a trust fund, with the income to be applied every fourth year to purchase a racing eight. It was proposed 'to affix in the successive boats a plate with a suitable inscription' in position 'two' of the boat, and to put a photograph of David Radcliffe in the barge.

> All Corpus men will thank Mr Radcliffe for his generosity in so materially assisting the Boat Club, and further, will feel deeply that he is helping us to perpetuate an inheritance bought not by money but by the lives of so many of our best and strongest. In our determination to restore the activities of peace, we must not forget the devoted self-sacrifice of the past members of our boat and our teams, who have not lived to enjoy the health and vigour of mind and body matured on the Isis and on our playing fields; and future generations may well draw inspiration from the memory of one who strove heartily for the College in his brief career, and hearkened to a higher calling of duty.[34]

A year later Mr and Mrs Radcliffe had increased the amount of this trust fund from the original £500 of 5 per-cent War Loan to £700, and gave an additional £60 cash to cover the expired value of Corpus's previous boat. Editors of the *Pelican Record* noted: 'To a small college the gift is particularly valuable, and so too, we may hope, will be the manifestation of our gratitude, if future crews maintain and amplify the honourable tradition of Corpus boats.'[35] During the year that Radcliffe spent at Corpus before the outbreak of war, he had been Acting Secretary of the Boat Club as well as rowing in the Eight, during which race Corpus started in 11th place and ended tenth. Clearly his parents felt that establishing the trust fund for Corpus Boat Club was a fitting tribute to their son.

The Maude Barge, opened with great aplomb 12 years after the Armistice, was dedicated to another Corpuscle who had died at the front, and to his father, also a Corpuscle. Louis Edward Joseph Maude (CCC 1910–14) was the only son of the Revd Joseph Hooper Maude (CCC 1871–5) and Louisa Frederica Grey (née Fuller). Louis had been educated at Trinity College, Glenalmond before coming up to Corpus in 1910, where he obtained a second in Literae Humaniores in 1914. At Corpus Maude had served as Secretary and later Captain of Hockey, Secretary and President of the Pelican Essay Club, Secretary and then President of the Owlets, and was active in the Boat Club. After leaving Oxford he sat his civil service exam in 1914. When the war broke out he undertook military service in France as 2nd lieutenant in the King's Own Yorkshire Light Infantry. He was killed in action at Fricourt during the first day of the Battle of the Somme, a fortnight shy of his 23rd birthday. 'Described as "true and faithful sons of Corpus" by Mrs Maude and Dr Cecily Maude, it was "to fix a last glimpse of Louis, so characteristic of both him and his father that the happy inspiration of a memorial barge" took shape.'[36] The opening of this new barge, described as 'attractive and comfortable', took place on 7 May 1930. It was a splendid affair with lunch laid on in Corpus Hall for 50 people, and with 150 assembled for the presentation. A tablet was erected over the barge's fireplace to commemorate the donors and 'the two Maudes in whose memory the barge stood'.[37] The June 1930 issue of the *Pelican Record* continues: 'after lunch guests made their way down to the riverbank where, amid much applause the barge was unlocked by Miss Maude, sister of Joseph, who had earlier been presented with the key'. The barge was recorded as the 'heroine of the occasion', being 'subjected to a severe test of buoyancy', her upper decks laden with supporters.[38] This barge was, as others, 'requisitioned under the emergency powers of 13 July [1943] by the Admiralty "for naval purposes"'.[39]

Christopher Bushell, VC (CCC 1906–9) had been an active member of Corpus, acting as Secretary and later Captain of the Boat Club, Secretary and then President of the Owlets, and had been the College Captain in 1908. He achieved a third in Modern History in 1909. Bushell subsequently pursued a military career, entering the Special Reserve of Officers, Queen's Regiment (Royal West Surrey Regiment) in 1912. He married Rachel Lambert in 1915; a daughter, Elisabeth Hope, was born to them in 1916. During the First World War Bushell served in France, where he was wounded twice. He was mentioned in dispatches in 1916 and 1917, obtained a Distinguished Service Order in 1918, and was awarded the Victoria Cross in March 1918. Bushell was killed in action near Morlancourt on 8 August 1918. He was later remembered fondly in the *Pelican Record*:

> The men of Bushell's year at Corpus were so united as to be called 'the Push'. Having discovered his powers on the River he became their acknowledged leader. It was customary then, and it may be again, for those who lodged in the front quad to find room daily in turn for all members of the College present at lunch. These heterogeneous banquets initiated the Freshmen into Corpus society, but it was Bushell's special genius to secure that their embarrassments did not completely overwhelm the tyro hosts. He knew how to exercise authority with tact and to smooth over the most painful situations. So it was at the College Dining Club and in other spheres of hospitality. It was to him that first anxious College authorities looked to preserve a semblance of decorum in the excitements of a College Bump Supper. They did not look in vain.[40]

After the war, the Christopher Bushell Prize of books, for Modern History undergraduates, was established at Corpus in 1923.[41] The prize continues to this day, awarded annually to the Corpus History student who obtains the highest mark in their dissertation in Finals.[42]

Geoffrey Bury Ramsbotham (CCC 1912–14) had arrived at Corpus as a Scholar in 1912, and undertook Jurisprudence Prelims before switching to Modern History during his second year. Less than a year after undertaking military service he was killed in action at Festubert near Ypres on 16 May 1915. Six months later, his bequest of a two-handled silver cup and cover reached Corpus, bearing the following inscription:

> This Cup was bequeathed to the President, Fellows, and Scholars of Corpus Christi College, Oxford, by Geoffrey Ramsbotham, Esq., Scholar of the same College 1912–1914, Lieut., 3rd Batt. Royal Sussex Regiment, August, 1914, attached 1st Batt. South Stafford-shire Regiment, December, 1914. Killed in action at Festubert in Flanders, May 16, 1915, aged 21.

This 14-inch cup, with its campana-shaped body engraved with Rams-botham's arms on one side and the College arms above the inscription on the other, remains in Corpus's possession to this day.[43] Writers in the *Pelican Record*'s issue for 1915 declared that 'the cup and its legend will keep alive the name of a brave man and a loyal son of Corpus'.[44] Ramsbotham's nephew later studied at Corpus in 1945–7, after serving in the Second World War.

William Hugh David de Pass (CCC 1911–14) was declared missing, believed killed in action at Pouzeau-Chaulnes on 25 March 1918, aged 25. During the year following his death, the young man's father wrote several letters to the College 'concerning a plan of commemorating the connexion with the College of his son, the late W. H. D. de Pass', which were read aloud by the President at a College Meeting in April 1919.[45] Six months later, plans were finalised, and the commemora-tion became a donation to the Junior Library. By Michaelmas Term 1919 the fund had been established, and books began to appear on the Library shelves. In the case of duplicates, the copies already in Corpus's possession were sold and replaced by those from the bequest. Mr Charles de Pass generously supplemented this legacy by a gift of £350 in his son's memory, for the purchase of further books for the Junior Library. Books bought under this gift bear a label with an inscription indicating the source from which they had been bought. 'The College owes a great debt to Mr de Pass for supplementing the resources of the Library at a time when the prices of books have increased: his gift has a self-perpetuating and increasing character that will keep alive the memory of the donor and his son in the minds of future generations of Corpus men who profit by it.'[46] During his three years at Corpus W. H. D. de Pass had played for Corpus's 1913–14 Rugby XV team, and had obtained a third in Classics Moderations. His memorial inscription can still be found in approximately one hundred volumes in the College Library.[47]

This influx of individual memorials to Corpus was in keeping with the pleas from the *Pelican* in 1919 for 'individual subscriptions to other needy objects'[48] within College. It appears that the overriding instinct of the time was to attempt to return to lives of pre-war normality, however superficial this might be; and the most profound sentiment behind such an attitude seems to have been that this was the best way to honour and remember friends, family and loved ones who had not returned from the battlefields. E. S. Craig and W. M. Gibson, editors of the University's *Roll of Service*, wrote poignantly of such notions in their introduction:

> Much thought has been expended, during the War and since, on the fittest way of honouring the dead. They will not come back, and we, who remember them and think of them, like to believe that they will always be remembered. But let us be just to them. They did not ask, when they gave their lives, that their memories should be preserved … Their virtue, which was a live thing, cannot be engraved on stone or printed in a book, but it still is here, to be sought for among other live things.[49]

ENDNOTES

1. Corpus's President and Fellows in Wartime

1. Thomas Charles-Edwards and Julian Reid, *Corpus Christi College, Oxford: A History* (Oxford, 2017), p. 313.
2. Ibid., p. 320.
3. *Pelican Record*, vol. 1, no. 1 (June 1891).
4. Charles-Edwards and Reid, *Corpus Christi College, Oxford*, p. 319.
5. Ibid., p. 360.
6. Christopher Platt, *The Most Obliging Man in Europe: Life and Times of the Oxford Scout* (London, 1986), p. 21.
7. Norma Aubertin-Porter, '"One servant is worth a thousand gadgets": Some Oxford College Servants 1700–1800', seminar given at All Souls College, 3 Nov. 2017.
8. Charles-Edwards and Reid, *Corpus Christi College, Oxford*, p. 325.
9. Ibid., p. 328.
10. CCCA/E/7/1: Tenterden Essay Club Minute Book, 1897–1904.
11. Charles-Edwards and Reid, *Corpus Christi College, Oxford*, p. 330.
12. *Pelican Record*, vol. 10, no. 1 (Dec. 1909).
13. *Pelican Record*, vol. 10, no. 3 (June 1910).
14. *Pelican Record*, vol. 10, no. 4 (Dec. 1910).
15. *Pelican Record*, vol. 11, no. 4 (Dec. 1912).
16. John Stevenson, 'Government, Oxford and Oriel, 1914–1990', in Jeremy Catto (ed.), *Oriel College: A History* (Oxford, 2013), p. 680.
17. J. M. Winter, 'Oxford and the First World War', in Brian Harrison (ed.), *The History of the University of Oxford*, vol. viii. *The Twentieth Century* (Oxford, 1994), p. 3.
18. Stevenson, 'Government, Oxford and Oriel, 1914–1990', p. 680.
19. *Pelican Record*, vol. 12, no. 2 (Mar. 1914).
20. Winter, 'Oxford and the First World War', p. 3.
21. *Pelican Record*, vol. 12, no. 4 (Dec. 1914).

22. G. B. Grundy, *Fifty-Five Years at Oxford: An Unconventional Autobiography* (London, 1945), p. 109.
23. Ibid., p. 110.
24. 'The Vice Chancellor's Speech 1914', *Oxford Magazine* (16 Oct. 1914), p. 8. With thanks to Professor Sir Brian Harrison, Corpus Emeritus Fellow, for this insight.
25. CCCA/B/17/4/2: Letters to President Case About War Service, 1914–18: Letter from Henry Le Blanc Lightfoot to Thomas Case, 5 Aug. 1914.
26. Ibid.: Letters from Case to Lightfoot, 6 and 8 Aug. 1914.
27. Grundy, *Fifty-Five Years at Oxford*, pp. 110–11.
28. Ibid., p. 110.
29. CCCA/B/14/1/1/36: President Case's Report on the War's Impact on Corpus, 1914.
30. CCCA/B/17/4/2: Letters to President Case About War Service, 1914–18: Letter from Radcliffe to Case, 11 Oct. 1915.
31. Ibid.: Letter from Ramsbotham to Case, 22 May 1915.
32. Ibid.: Letter from Brown to Janasz, 22 June 1915.
33. Ibid.: Letter from J. F. Hayes to Case, undated.
34. Ibid.: Letter from J. L. Palon to Case, 17 Dec. 1915.
35. Ibid.: Letter from H. G. Willink to Case, 29 Apr. 1918.
36. L. W. B. Brockliss, Matthew D'Ancona, Robin Darwall-Smith and Andrew Hegarty, '"Everyone of us is a Magdalen Man": The College, 1854–1928', in L. W. B. Brockliss (ed.), *Magdalen College Oxford: A History* (Oxford, 2008), pp. 560–2.
37. CCCA/B/17/4/2: Letters to President Case About War Service, 1914–18: Letter from Mowat to Case, 17 Aug. 1914.
38. CCCA/B/14/1/1/36: Case's Report on the War's Impact on Corpus, 1914.
39. CCCA/B/17/4/2: Letters to President Case About War Service, 1914–18: Letter from Grundy to Case, 30 Aug. 1914.
40. CCCA/B/14/1/1/36: Case's Report on the War's Impact on Corpus, 1914.
41. Ibid.
42. Thomas Case, *Letters to 'The Times' 1884–1922* (Oxford, 1927), p. 160.
43. *Pelican Record*, vol. 12, no. 4 (Dec. 1914).
44. *Pelican Record*, vol. 13, no. 4 (Dec. 1916).
45. *Pelican Record*, vol. 14, no. 4 (June 1919).
46. Malcolm Graham, *Oxford in the Great War* (Barnsley, 2014), pp. 32–3.
47. Ibid., p. 55.
48. *Pelican Record*, vol. 14, no. 5 (Dec. 1919).
49. *Pelican Record*, vol. 13, no. 2 (Mar. 1916).
50. Grundy, *Fifty-Five Years at Oxford*, pp. 130–1.
51. *Pelican Record*, vol. 13, no. 2 (Mar. 1916).

52. Grundy, *Fifty-Five Years at Oxford*, p. 134.
53. Ibid., p. 130.
54. P. A. Hunt (comp.) and N. A. Flanagan (ed.), *Corpus Christi College Biographical Register 1880–1974* (Oxford, 1988), pp. 229 and 380.
55. *Pelican Record*, vol. 13, no. 1 (Dec. 1915).
56. CCCA/B/4/1/12: College Meeting Minute Book, 11 Oct. 1916 – 19 June 1923: 17 Jan. 1919.
57. Hunt (comp.) and Flanagan (ed.), *Corpus Christi College Biographical Register 1880–1974*, p. 30.
58. *Pelican Record*, vol. 13, no. 1 (Dec. 1915).
59. Radley College Archives: *The Radleian*, no. 419 (15 Dec. 1917).
60. CCC MS 472: Biography and Account of the Death of George Willink, revised Jan. 1919, accompanying letter from H. G. Willink to Sir Richard Winn Livingstone, Dec. 1922.
61. CCCA/B/4/1/11: College Meeting Minute Book, 28 Oct. 1907 – 20 June 1916: 10 Oct. 1914.
62. Ibid., 12 June 1915, 13 Nov. 1915 and 29 Apr. 1916.
63. CCCA/B/4/1/12: College Meeting Minute Book, 11 Oct. 1916 – 19 June 1923: 30 Nov. 1918.
64. Ibid., 10 Nov. 1917.
65. Ibid.: 14 Oct. 1916, 15 June 1918 and 30 Nov. 1918.
66. CCCA/B/4/1/11: College Meeting Minute Book, 28 Oct. 1907 – 20 June 1916: 16 Oct. 1915.
67. *Pelican Record*, vol. 13, no. 1 (Dec. 1915).
68. CCCA/B/4/1/12: College Meeting Minute, 11 Oct. 1916 – 19 June 1923: 30 Nov. 1918.
69. CCCA/B/4/1/11: College Meeting Minute Book, 28 Oct. 1907 – 20 June 1916: 10 Oct. 1914, 21 Nov. 1914, 22 May 1915 and 13 Nov. 1915.
70. CCCA/B/4/1/12: College Meeting Minute Book, 11 Oct. 1916 – 19 June 1923: 14 Oct. 1916 and 10 Nov. 1917.
71. Ibid., 15 June 1918 and 31 May 1919.
72. *Pelican Record*, vol. 13, no. 5 (Mar. 1917).
73. Graham, *Oxford in the Great War*, p. 93.
74. CCCA/B/4/1/12: College Meeting Minute Book, 11 Oct. 1916 – 19 June 1923: 17 Feb. 1917, 15 June 1918 and 30 Nov. 1918.

2. Corpus at the Front

1. See J. M. Winter, 'Oxford and the First World War', in Brian Harrison (ed.), *The History of the University of Oxford*, vol. viii. *The Twentieth Century* (Oxford, 1994), pp. 19–20.

2. The author has calculated these casualty and service rates from E. S. Craig and W. M. Gibson (eds.), *Oxford University Roll of Service* (Oxford, 1920); *Pelican Record* (1914–19); P. A. Hunt (comp.) and N. A. Flanagan (ed.), *Corpus Christi College Biographical Register 1880–1974* (Oxford, 1988) and other archive sources.

3. Winter, 'Oxford and the First World War', p. 19; and John Maddicott, '"An Infinitesimal Part in Armageddon": Exeter College and the First World War', *Exeter College Register* (2017), p. 58.

4. Winter, 'Oxford and the First World War', p. 19.

5. See <http://www.ccc.ox.ac.uk/Roll-of-Honour-1914–1918/>. A physical copy is also available to view in Corpus Christi College Chapel, and at the Lodge.

6. CCCA/B/17/4/2: Letters to President Case About War Service, 1914–18: Letter from William Griffiths to Thomas Case, undated.

7. The King's School, Worcester Archives: *The Vigornian*, vol. 8, no. 86 (July 1916).

8. With thanks to Lesley Wood, Librarian, Archivist and Information Manager at Bedford School, for this information.

9. Wellington School Archives: Register, 1859–1948, and *The Wellingtonian*, vol. 23, no. 11 (1917).

10. CCCA/E/5/4: Pelican Essay Club Minute Book, 1910–14: 27 Jan. 1911.

11. A copy of this volume can be found in Corpus Library.

12. Harold Leslie Rayner, *Letters from France by Harold Leslie Rayner, July 26 1915 to June 30 1916: Selected by His Mother and Printed for Private Circulation* (London, 1919), pp. 14–15: 27 July 1915.

13. Ibid., p. 28: 9 Aug. 1915.

14. Ibid., p. 45: 29 Aug. 1915.

15. Ibid., p. 36: 18 Aug. 1915.

16. Ibid., pp. 50–1: 5 Sept. 1915.

17. Ibid., p. 67: 2 Oct. 1915.

18. Ibid., pp. 70–1: 8 Oct 1915.

19. Ibid., pp. 116, 119 and 121: 23 and 26 Dec. 1915 and 2 Jan. 1916.

20. Ibid., pp. 183–4: 12 Apr. 1916.

21. Ibid., pp. 211–12: 22 June 1916.

22. Ibid., p. 217: 29 June 1916.

23. Ibid., p. 218: 30 June 1916.

24. Merve Goddard, Brenda Collins and Mary Hallett, *For God, School & Country: The Upcotts of Christ's Hospital 1902 to 1919* (Netherbury, 2017), p. 100.

25. *Pelican Record*, vol. 13, no. 4 (Dec. 1916).

26. Rayner, *Letters from France by Harold Leslie Rayner*, Foreword, p. 4.

27. CCCA/E/6/7: Owlet Club Minute Book, 1907–9: undated 459th meeting, 1909.

28. Ibid.: undated 461st meeting, 1909.

29. Ibid.: undated 474th and 475th meetings, 1909.

30. CCCA/E/6/8: Owlet Club Minute Book, 1909–11: 21 Nov. 1909.

31. Donald Hankey, *Letters of Donald Hankey 'A Student in Arms'*, with introduction and notes by Edward Miller (2nd edn., London, 1919), p. 311.

32. Ross Davies, *'A Student in Arms': Donald Hankey and Edwardian Society at War* (Abingdon, 2016), p. ix.

33. A copy can be found in Corpus Library.

34. Hankey, *Letters of Donald Hankey*, p. 363: 2 May 1915.

35. Donald Hankey, *A Student in Arms* (17th edn., London, 1917), p. 235.

36. Davies, *Donald Hankey and Edwardian Society at War*, p. 4.

37. Hankey, *A Student in Arms*, pp. 60–6.

38. Davies, *Donald Hankey and Edwardian Society at War*, p. 2.

39. Hankey, *A Student in Arms*, p. 202.

40. Davies, *Donald Hankey and Edwardian Society at War*, p. 47.

41. Hankey, *A Student in Arms*, pp. 206–9.

42. Ibid., p. 5.

43. Maddicott, '"An Infinitesimal Part in Armageddon": Exeter College and the First World War', p. 61.

44. Richard Symonds, 'Letters of R. W. Dugdale, 1915–1918', in *Raising the Ladder: Further Worthies and Noteworthies of Corpus Christi College, Oxford* (Oxford, 2008), p. 102.

45. CCC MS 608: R. W. Dugdale Letters, 1915–18, p. 8: 4 Oct. 1915.

46. Ibid., p. 22: 2 Nov. 1915.

47. Ibid., p. 10: 13 Oct. 1915.

48. Ibid., pp. 64 and 71: 22 Aug. and 15 Oct. 1916.

49. Ibid., p. 82: 3 Dec. 1916.

50. Ibid., pp. 189 and 136: 18 Aug. 1918 and 1 Sept. 1917.

51. Symonds, 'Letters of R. W. Dugdale', p. 103.

52. CCC MS 608: R. W. Dugdale Letters, 1915–18, p. 103: 3 Mar 1917.

53. Ibid., p. 109: 14 Apr. 1917.

54. Symonds, 'Letters of R. W. Dugdale', p. 103.

55. CCC MS 608: R. W. Dugdale Letters, 1915–18, p. 98: 22 Feb. 1917.

56. Ibid., p. 148: 23 Oct. 1917.

57. Ibid., pp. 155 and 171: 21 Nov. 1917 and 15 Mar. 1918.

58. Symonds, 'Letters of R. W. Dugdale', p. 104.

59. CCC MS 608: R. W. Dugdale Letters, 1915–18, p. 197: 13 Oct. 1918.

60. Symonds, 'Letters of R. W. Dugdale', p. 105.

61. CCC MS 608: R. W. Dugdale Letters, 1915–18, p. 202: 11 July 1919.

62. Ibid.: Dec. 1918.
63. CCCA/E/2/1/2: JCR Minute Book, 1910–33.
64. Hunt (comp.) and Flanagan (ed.), *Corpus Christi College Biographical Register 1880–1974*, p. 219.
65. Ibid., pp. 188–9.
66. Ibid, p. 156.
67. *Pelican Record*, vol. 13, no. 1 (Dec. 1915).
68. *Pelican Record*, vol. 13, no. 5 (Mar. 1917).
69. *Pelican Record*, vol. 14, no. 1 (Dec. 1917).
70. The Sidgwick Prize still exists, in recent years split into separate undergraduate and graduate prizes. The graduate prize is in the original style, a cash prize from the fund established by Arthur Sidgwick (CCC Fellow 1882–1902 and 1904–20) for essays by graduate members on either 'some aspect of the History of the College, its members, or its possessions'; the 'significant and substantial contribution' of a graduate's thesis; or 'the single most important thing you have learnt as a graduate student'. With thanks to Rachel Clifford, Corpus Academic Registrar, for this information.
71. CCCA/B/17/4/2: Letters to President Case About War Service, 1914–18: Letters from Hale to Case, 7 and 11 Aug. 1914, and from Mrs Hale to Case, 1 Nov. 1914.
72. *Pelican Record*, vol. 14, no. 1 (Dec. 1917).
73. *Pelican Record*, vol. 14, no. 4 (June 1919).
74. *Pelican Record*, vol. 14, no. 2 (June 1918).
75. Craig and Gibson (eds.), *Oxford University Roll of Service*.
76. Judith Curthoys, *The Cardinal's College: Christ Church, Chapter and Verse* (London, 2012), pp. 300–1.
77. With thanks to Hannah Morgan, Corpus Senior Library Assistant, for this information.
78. *Pelican Record*, vol. 14, no. 5 (Dec. 1919).
79. Peggy Attlee, *With a Quiet Conscience: A Biography of Thomas Simons Attlee* (London, 1995), p. 67.
80. John Bew, *Citizen Clem: A Biography of Attlee* (London, 2016), p. 78.
81. Attlee, *With a Quiet Conscience*, p. 55.
82. Ibid., pp. 49–51.
83. Ibid., pp. 55–6.
84. Ibid., p. 61.
85. Ibid., pp. 62–3.
86. Ibid., p. 64.
87. Ibid., p. 66.
88. Ibid., p. 66.
89. *Pelican Record*, vol. 14, no. 4 (June 1919).

90. Attlee, *With a Quiet Conscience*, pp. 67–8.
91. E. L. Woodward, *Short Journey* (London, 1942), p. 117.
92. With thanks to Brian Harrison for this insight.

3. Corpus Servants in Wartime

1. Research undertaken by Liz Woolley, May 2017, with thanks to Stephanie Jenkins (<www.oxfordhistory.org.uk/war/stfrideswide>) and Emma Hill.
2. *Pelican Record*, vol. 12, no. 4 (Dec. 1914).
3. Research undertaken by Liz Woolley, May 2017.
4. *Pelican Record*, vol. 13, no. 1 (Dec. 1915).
5. *Pelican Record,* vol. 13, no. 3 (June 1916).
6. Research undertaken by Liz Woolley, May 2017.
7. Research undertaken by Liz Woolley, May 2017.
8. CCCA/B/4/7/1B: Servants' Committee Minute Book, 1897–1932: 2 Mar. 1903 and 1 Nov. 1918.
9. Research undertaken by Liz Woolley, May 2017.
10. CCCA/B/4/7/1B: Servants' Committee Minute Book, 1897–1932: 10 Sept. 1912.
11. Brian Harrison, 'College Servants in Corpus Forty Years Ago', *Pelican Record*, vol. 45 (Dec. 2010), p. 12.
12. Research undertaken by Liz Woolley, May 2017.
13. CCCA/B/4/7/1B: Servants' Committee Minute Book, 1897–1932: 14 Oct. 1913.
14. Christopher Platt, *The Most Obliging Man in Europe: Life and Times of the Oxford Scout* (London, 1986), p. 88.
15. *Pelican Record*, vol. 12, no. 4 (Dec. 1914).
16. CCCA/B/4/7/1B: Servants' Committee Minute Book, 1897–1932: 2 Sept. 1919.
17. Ibid.: 15 Feb. 1909 and 29 Oct. 1913.
18. *Pelican Record*, vol. 12, no. 4 (Dec. 1914).
19. *Pelican Record*, vol. 14, no. 2 (June 1918).
20. CCCA/B/3/6: 'White Books', Annual Lists of College Members, Michaelmas Term 1929.
21. CCCA/B/4/7/1B: Servants' Committee Minute Book, 1897–1932: 10 Mar. 1905, 21 Feb. 1905 and 21 Feb, 1914.
22. *Pelican Record*, vol. 13, no. 3 (June 1916).
23. *Pelican Record*, vol. 13, no. 6 (June 1917).
24. CCCA/B/4/7/1B: Servants' Committee Minute Book, 1897–1932: 1 Apr. 1919.
25. Quoted from B. W. Robinson to B. Harrison, 20 July 1989, in Harrison, 'College Servants in Corpus Forty Years Ago', p. 24.

26. CCCA/B/3/6: 'White Books', Annual Lists of College Members, Michaelmas Term 1929.
27. *Pelican Record*, vol. 13, no. 3 (June 1916).
28. *Pelican Record*, vol. 14, no. 4 (June 1919).
29. *Pelican Record*, vol. 13, no. 5 (Mar. 1917).
30. *Pelican Record*, vol. 13, no. 3 (June 1916).
31. *Pelican Record*, vol. 13, no. 1 (Dec. 1915).
32. Ibid.
33. *Pelican Record*, vol. 13, no. 3 (June 1916).
34. *Pelican Record*, vol. 12, no. 6 (June 1915).
35. CCCA/B/4/7/1B: Servants' Committee Minute Book, 1897–1932: 21 June 1909 and 8 Jan. 1914.
36. *Pelican Record*, vol. 12, no. 4 (Dec. 1914).
37. CCCA/B/4/7/1B: Servants' Committee Minute Book, 1897–1932: 9 and 18 June 1919.
38. Ibid.: 7 Oct. 1907, 8 Feb. 1909 and 23 Mar. 1911.
39. Platt, *The Most Obliging Man in Europe*, p. 21.
40. *Pelican Record*, vol. 12, no. 4 (Dec. 1914).
41. *Pelican Record*, vol. 14, no. 3 (Dec. 1918).
42. CCCA/B/4/7/1B: Servants' Committee Minute Book, 1897–1932: 1 May 1903, 7 Oct. 1907, 23 Mar. 1911 and 14 Oct. 1913.
43. *Pelican Record*, vol. 13, no. 3 (June 1916).
44. *Pelican Record*, vol. 13, no. 6 (June 1917).
45. CCCA/B/4/7/1B: Servants' Committee Minute Book, 1897–1932: 1 Apr. 1919.
46. Ibid.: 10 Feb. 1905, 17 June 1910 and 10 Oct. 1914.
47. *Pelican Record*, vol. 13, no. 4 (Dec. 1916).
48. *Pelican Record*, vol. 12, no. 2 (Mar. 1914).
49. CCCA/B/4/7/1B: Servants' Committee Minute Book, 1897–1932: 14 Oct. 1913.
50. Ibid.: 29 Oct. 1913.
51. Ibid.: 10 Oct. 1914.
52. Ibid.: 7 Nov. 1914.
53. CCCA/B/4/1/11: College Meeting Minute Book, 28 Oct. 1907 – 20 June 1916: 21 Nov. 1914.
54. CCCA/B/4/7/1B: Servants' Committee Minute Book, 1897–1932: 15 May 1916.
55. Harrison, 'College Servants in Corpus Forty Years Ago', p. 11.
56. CCCA/B/4/7/1B: Servants' Committee Minute Book, 1897–1932: 15 May 1916.
57. Ibid.: 10 Feb. 1905.

58. Ibid.: 17 Mar. 1904.
59. Ibid.: 8 Dec. 1917.
60. CCCA/B/3/6: 'White Books', Annual Lists of College Members, Michaelmas Term 1929.
61. Harrison, 'College Servants in Corpus Forty Years Ago', p. 29.
62. CCCA/B/3/6: 'White Books', Annual Lists of College Members, Michaelmas Term 1929.
63. 'Supplement to the Catalogue of Presidents, Fellows, Scholars, Chaplains, Exhibitioners, Commoners, Etc. of Corpus Christi College, 1903–1912', *Pelican Record*, vol. 11, no. 6 (June 1913).
64. CCCA/B/4/7/1B: Servants' Committee Minute Book, 1897–1932: 18 June 1912.
65. CCCA/B/3/6: 'White Books', Annual Lists of College Members, Michaelmas Term 1929.
66. CCCA/B/4/7/1B: Servant's Committee Minute Book, 1897–1932: 8 Dec. 1917.
67. Ibid.: 21 June 1918.
68. Ibid.: 1 Nov. 1918.
69. Ibid.: 1 Apr. 1919.
70. Ibid.: Michaelmas Term 1904.
71. Ibid.: 15 Mar. 1919.
72. Ibid.: 1 Apr. 1919.
73. CCCA/B/4/1/12: College Meeting Minute Book, 11 Oct. 1916 – 19 June 1923: 21 June 1919.
74. Ibid.: 21 June 1919.
75. P. A. Hunt (comp.) and N. A. Flanagan (ed.), *Corpus Christi College Oxford Biographical Register, 1880–1974* (Oxford, 1988), pp. 61–2.
76. CCCA/B/4/7/1B: Servants' Committee Minute Book, 1897–1932: 19 Nov. 1919.
77. CCCA/B/4/1/12: College Meeting Minute Book, 11 Oct. 1916 – 19 June 1923: 14 Feb. 1920.
78. CCCA/B/4/7/1B: Servants' Committee Minute Book, 1897–1932: 19 Nov. 1919.
79. CCCA/B/4/1/12: College Meeting Minute Book, 11 Oct. 1916 – 19 June 1923: 19 Nov. 1919.

4. Corpus Life and Buildings in Wartime

1. E. S. Craig and W. M. Gibson (eds.), *Oxford University Roll of Service* (Oxford, 1920), pp. 5–7.
2. CCCA/B/4/1/11: College Meeting Minute Book, 28 Oct. 1907 – 20 June 1916: 21 Nov. 1914.

3. *Pelican Record*, vol. 12, no. 5 (Mar. 1915).

4. CCCA/B/17/4/2: Letters to President Case About War Service, 1914–18: Draft letter from Thomas Case, 25 Feb. 1915.

5. Ibid.: Letter from Newton-King to Case, 27 Feb. 1915.

6. CCCA/B/4/1/11: College Meeting Minute Book, 28 Oct. 1907 – 20 June 1916: 13 Feb. 1915.

7. Ibid.: 6 Mar. 1915.

8. *Pelican Record*, vol. 12, no. 5 (Mar. 1915).

9. CCCA/B/4/1/11: College Meeting Minute Book, 28 Oct. 1907 – 20 June 1916: 20 June 1916.

10. CCCA/B/4/1/12: College Meeting Minute Book, 11 Oct. 1916 – 19 June 1923: 14 Oct. 1916.

11. *Pelican Record*, vol. 13, no. 4 (Dec. 1916).

12. CCCA/B/4/1/12: College Meeting Minute Book, 11 Oct. 1916 – 19 June 1923: 11 Oct. 1916.

13. *Pelican Record*, vol. 13, no. 5 (Mar. 1917).

14. *Pelican Record*, vol. 13, no. 4 (Dec. 1916).

15. CCCA/B/4/1/12: College Meeting Minute Book, 11 Oct. 1916 – 19 June 1923: 10 Oct. 1917.

16. Ibid.: 10 Oct. 1917.

17. Ibid.: 19 Jan. 1918.

18. Ibid.: 9 Nov 1918.

19. Malcolm Graham, *Oxford in the Great War* (Barnsley, 2014), p. 112.

20. CCCA/B/4/1/12: College Meeting Minute Book, 11 Oct. 1916 – 19 June 1923: 30 Nov. 1918.

21. CCCA/B/4/1/11: College Meeting Minute Book, 28 Oct. 1907 – 20 June 1916: 22 May 1915.

22. Ibid.: 13 Nov. 1915.

23. Ibid.: 4 Dec. 1915.

24. Ibid.: 5 Feb. 1916.

25. *Pelican Record*, vol. 12, no. 4 (Dec. 1914).

26. *Pelican Record*, vol. 14, no. 2 (June 1918).

27. *Pelican Record*, vol. 14, no. 3 (Dec. 1918).

28. *Pelican Record*, vol. 14, no. 4 (June 1919).

29. Ibid.

30. P. A. Hunt (comp.) and N. A. Flanagan (ed.), *Corpus Christi College Oxford Biographical Register 1880–1974* (Oxford, 1988), pp. 256–70.

31. 'The Illustrated First World War from the Archives of *The Illustrated London News*: Food and Rationing', <https://www.illustratedfirstworldwar.com/topics/food-and-rationing/>, 17 Oct. 2017.

32. CCCA/B/4/1/12: College Meeting Minute Book, 11 Oct. 1916 – 19 June 1923: 17 Feb. 1917.

33. *Pelican Record*, vol. 13, no. 5 (Mar. 1917).

34. CCCA/B/4/1/12: College Meeting Minute Book, 11 Oct. 1916 – 19 June 1923: 26 May 1917.

35. Ibid.: 8 Dec. 1917.

36. J. M. Winter, 'Oxford and the First World War', in Brian Harrison (ed.), *The History of the University of Oxford*, vol. viii. *The Twentieth Century* (Oxford, 1994), p. 12.

37. Graham, *Oxford in the Great War*, p. 104.

38. CCCA/B/4/1/12: College Meeting Minute Book, 11 Oct. 1916 – 19 June 1923: 8 Dec. 1917.

39. Ibid.: 9 Feb. 1918.

40. Ibid.: 27 Apr. 1918.

41. Ibid.: 17 Jan. 1919.

42. Ibid.: 9 Feb. 1918.

43. Ibid.: 25 May 1918.

44. Ibid.: 10 Oct. 1918.

45. Ibid.: 30 Nov. 1918.

46. *Pelican Record*, vol. 14, no. 3 (Dec. 1918).

47. Winter, 'Oxford and the First World War', p. 12.

48. CCCA/B/4/1/11: College Meeting Minute Book, 28 Oct. 1907 – 20 June 1916: 13 Feb. 1915.

49. Ibid.: 22 May 1915.

50. Ibid.: 19 May 1916.

51. CCCA/B/4/1/11: College Meeting Minute Book, 28 Oct. 1907 – 20 June 1916: 22 May 1915 and 29 Apr. 1916; CCCA/B/4/1/12: College Meeting Minute Book, 11 Oct. 1916 – 19 June 1923: 26 May 1917 and 15 June 1918.

52. CCCA/B/4/1/11: College Meeting Minute Book, 28 Oct. 1907 – 20 June 1916: 29 Apr. 1916.

53. CCCA/B/4/1/11: College Meeting Minute Book, 28 Oct. 1907 – 20 June 1916: 22 May 1915 and 5 Feb. 1916; CCCA/B/4/1/12: College Meeting Minute Book, 11 Oct. 1916 – 19 June 1923: 26 May 1917.

54. CCCA/B/4/1/12: College Meeting Minute Book, 11 Oct. 1916 – 19 June 1923: 2 Dec. 1916.

55. Ibid.: 17 Feb. 1917.

56. Ibid.: 19 Oct. 1918.

57. Ibid.: 8 Feb. 1919.

58. *Pelican Record*, vol. 12, no. 4 (Dec. 1914).

59. *Pelican Record*, vol. 12, no. 5 (Mar. 1915).

60. *Pelican Record*, vol. 12, no. 6 (June 1915).

61. Ibid.
62. *Pelican Record*, vol. 13, no. 3 (June 1916).
63. *Pelican Record*, vol. 13, no. 4 (Dec. 1916).
64. *Pelican Record*, vol. 14, no. 1 (Dec. 1917).
65. *Pelican Record*, vol. 14, no. 2 (June 1918).
66. CCCA/B/4/1/11: College Meeting Minute Book, 28 Oct. 1907 – 20 June 1916: 13 Feb. 1915.
67. CCCA/B/4/1/12: College Meeting Minute Book, 11 Oct. 1916 – 19 June 1923: 14 Oct. 1916.
68. *Pelican Record*, vol. 13, no. 4 (Dec. 1916).
69. CCCA/B/4/1/12: College Meeting Minute Book, 11 Oct. 1916 – 19 June 1923: 26 May 1917.
70. Ibid.: 10 Nov. 1917.
71. CCCA/Bridges/C/3/1/12/15: Letters 1910–30: Letter to Robert Bridges from Edward Talbot, 21 Aug. 1929.
72. Clare Hopkins, *Trinity: 450 Years of an Oxford College Community* (Oxford, 2005), p. 356.
73. *Pelican Record*, vol. 14, no. 5 (Dec. 1919).
74. *Pelican Record*, vol. 14, no. 4 (June 1919).
75. *Pelican Record*, vol. 14, no. 6 (Mar. 1920).
76. CCCA/B/19/1/1: Gaudy Book, 1898–1946: War Service Dinner, 20 Apr. 1920.
77. Ibid.: Commemoration Dinner, 5 Oct. 1920.
78. *Pelican Record*, vol. 15, no. 1 (Dec. 1920).

Afterword: Corpus After the Armistice

1. Brian Harrison (ed.), *Corpuscles: A History of Corpus Christi College, Oxford in the Twentieth Century, Written by Its Members* (Oxford, 1994), p. 4: F. S. V. Donnison, 1919.
2. Quoted in Malcolm Graham, *Oxford in the Great War* (Barnsley, 2014), pp. 143–4.
3. Judith Curthoys, *The Cardinal's College: Christ Church, Chapter and Verse* (London, 2012), p. 301.
4. G. B. Grundy, *Fifty-Five Years at Oxford: An Unconventional Autobiography* (London, 1945), p. 137.
5. Quoted in Graham, *Oxford in the Great War*, p. 144.
6. CCCA/B/4/1/12: College Meeting Minute Book, 11 Oct. 1916 – 19 June 1923: 5 Mar. 1919.
7. Ibid.: 31 May 1919.
8. Curthoys, *Cardinal's College*, p. 302.
9. John Stevenson, 'The College Community, 1905–1950', in Jeremy Catto (ed.), *Oriel College: A History* (Oxford, 2013), p. 724.

10. *Pelican Record*, vol. 14, no. 4 (June 1919).

11. CCCA/B/14/1/1/19: War Memorial Design and Set-Up Papers 1920–1: Letter from W. P. Ker to Thomas Case, 5 June 1920.

12. Ibid.: Report of Committee, 16 June 1920.

13. Ibid.: Letter from Grundy to Case, 17 June 1920.

14. CCCA/B/4/1/12: College Meeting Minute Book, 11 Oct. 1916 – 19 June 1923: 19 June 1920.

15. CCCA/B/14/1/1/19: War Memorial Design and Set-Up Papers 1920–1: Letter from Livingstone to Case, 31 Aug. 1920.

16. With thanks to Professor Stephen Harrison, Corpus Mynors and Charles Oldham Fellow and Tutor in Latin, Professor of Latin Literature, for this translation.

17. CCCA/B/14/1/1/19: War Memorial Design and Set-Up Papers 1920–1: Report of the Committee of the War Memorial, 21 Jan. 1921.

18. Ibid.: Letter from Barnes to Case, 27 July 1921.

19. With thanks to Julian Reid, Merton College and Corpus Christi College Archivist, for this information.

20. L. W. B. Brockliss, Matthew D'Ancona, Robin Darwall-Smith and Andrew Hegarty, '"Everyone of us is a Magdalen Man": The College, 1854–1928', in L. W. B. Brockliss (ed.), *Magdalen College Oxford: A History* (Oxford, 2008), p. 562.

21. CCCA/B/4/1/12: College Meeting Minute Book, 11 Oct. 1916 – 19 June 1923: 14 Feb. 1920.

22. *Pelican Record*, vol. 14, no. 6 (Mar. 1920).

23. CCCA/Bridges/D/5/1/2/26: Papers from English Professors: Letter from Cyril Bailey to Robert Bridges, 21 Oct. 1920.

24. CCCA/Bridges/D/5/1/1/5: Papers from German Professors: Letter from Walter Horn to Bridges, 9 Nov. 1920.

25. CCCA/Bridges/D/5/1/2/12: Letter from Oscar Browning to Bridges, 28 Oct. 1920.

26. CCCA/B/4/1/11: College Meeting Minute Book 28 Oct. 1907 – 20 June 1916: 13 Feb. 1915.

27. Ibid.: 3 June 1916.

28. *Pelican Record*, vol. 13, no. 2 (Mar. 1916).

29. With thanks to Stephen Harrison for this translation.

30. *Pelican Record*, vol. 14, no. 6 (Mar. 1920).

31. P. A. Hunt (comp.) and N. A. Flanagan (ed.), *Corpus Christi College Oxford Biographical Register 1880–1974* (Oxford 1988), p. 207.

32. With thanks to Rachel Clifford, Corpus Academic Registrar, for this information.

33. CCCA/B/4/1/12: College Meeting Minute Book, 11 Oct. 1916 – 19 June 1923: 14 Feb. 1920.
34. *Pelican Record*, vol. 14, no. 6 (Mar. 1920).
35. *Pelican Record*, vol. 15, no. 2 (Mar. 1921).
36. Clare Sherriff, *The Oxford College Barges: Their History, Architecture and Use* (London, 2003), pp. 68–9.
37. Ibid., p. 69.
38. *Pelican Record*, vol. 19, no. 6 (June 1930).
39. Sherriff, *The Oxford College Barges*, p. 69.
40. *Pelican Record*, vol. 14, no. 3 (Dec. 1918).
41. Hunt (comp.) and Flanagan (ed.), *Corpus Christi College Oxford Biographical Register 1880–1974*, p. 201.
42. With thanks to Rachel Clifford for this information.
43. With thanks to Andy Rolfe, Corpus Domestic Bursar, for this information.
44. *Pelican Record*, vol. 13, no. 1 (Dec. 1915).
45. CCCA/B/4/1/12: College Meeting Minute Book, 11 Oct. 1916 – 19 June 1923: 26 Apr. 1919.
46. *Pelican Record*, vol. 14, no. 5 (Dec. 1919).
47. With thanks to Hannah Morgan, Corpus Senior Library Assistant, for this information.
48. *Pelican Record*, vol. 14, no. 4 (June 1919).
49. E. S. Craig and W. M. Gibson (eds.), *Oxford University Roll of Service* (Oxford, 1920), pp. xiv–xv.

ILLUSTRATIONS

1. Corpus Christi College Front Quad, c.1911. Reproduced by permission of the family of J. D. Upcott.

2. Corpus 23rd President, Thomas Case. © Oxfordshire County Council, Oxfordshire History Centre.

3. CCC Boat Club VIII, 1909. Reproduced by permission of the President and Fellows of Corpus Christi College, Oxford.

4. CCC Pelican Essay Club, 1910. Reproduced by permission of the President and Fellows of Corpus Christi College, Oxford.

5. CCC Rugby XV, 1913–14. Reproduced by permission of the President and Fellows of Corpus Christi College, Oxford.

6. RAF cadets in the Front Quad, May 1918. Reproduced by permission of the President and Fellows of Corpus Christi College, Oxford.

7. The Haigh memorial, Corpus Cloisters. Reproduced by permission of the President and Fellows of Corpus Christi College, Oxford.

8. Henry George Ward. Taken from the *Oxford Journal Illustrated*, 9 Sep 1916. The original newspaper is archived in the Oxfordshire History Centre.

9. Alfred William Clifford. Taken from the *Oxford Journal Illustrated*, 20 Oct 1915. The original newspaper is archived in the Oxfordshire History Centre.

10. Letter to President Thomas Case from R. B. Ramsbotham, 22 May 1915. Reproduced by permission of the President and Fellows of Corpus Christi College, Oxford.

11. Corpus Christi College First World War memorial. Reproduced by permission of the President and Fellows of Corpus Christi College, Oxford.

12. Corpus Christi College Front Quad. Reproduced by permission of the President and Fellows of Corpus Christi College, Oxford.

BIBLIOGRAPHY

Archives and Manuscripts

CCCA/B/3/6: 'White Books' Annual Lists of College Members, Michaelmas
Term 1929

CCCA/B/4/1/11: College Meeting Minute Book, 28 Oct. 1907 – 20 June 1916

CCCA/B/4/1/12: College Meeting Minute Book, 11 Oct. 1916 – 19 June 1923

CCCA/B/4/7/1B: Servants' Committee Minute Book, 1897–1932

CCCA/B/14/1/1/19: War Memorial Design and Set-Up Papers, 1920–1

CCCA/B/14/1/1/36: President Case's Report on the War's Impact on Corpus,
1914

CCCA/B/17/4/2: Letters to President Case About War Service, 1914–18

CCCA/B/19/1/1: Gaudy Book, 1898–1946

CCCA/C/50/4: College Finance, 1910–15

CCCA/D/10/1: List of Missing Books, 1879–c.1933

CCCA/E/2/1/2: JCR Minute Book, 1910–33

CCCA/E/3/1/3–4: Boat Club Captain's Books, 1898–1930

CCCA/E/4/2/1: Sundial Society Minute Book, 1910–22

CCCA/E/5/4: Pelican Essay Club Minute Book, 1910–14

CCCA/E/6/8–9: Owlet Club Minute Books, 1909–14

CCCA/E/7/1: Tenterden Minute Book, 1897–1904

CCCA/E/8/1: Wasps Dining Club Minute Book, 1900–1914

CCCA/Bridges/C/3/1/12/15: Letters, c.1910–30

CCCA/Bridges/D/5/1: Assorted German Reconciliation Papers, 1920–1

CCC MS 472: Biography and Account of the Death of George Willink, revised
January 1919

CCC MS 608: R. W. Dugdale Letters, 1915–18

The Pelican Record, 1891, 1909–22, 1930

The King's School, Worcester, Archives: Register, 1854–1948

Wellington School Archives: Register, 1859–1948

The Ousel: The Journal of Bedford Grammar School, 1912–14

The Radleian, the magazine of Radley College, No. 419, 15 December 1917

The Vigornian, the magazine of The King's School, Worcester, No. 86, Vol. VIII, July 1916

Wellingtonian, the magazine of Wellington School, Vol. 23, No. 11, 1917

Published Sources

Peggy Attlee, *With a Quiet Conscience: A Biography of Thomas Simons Attlee* (London, 1995)

Norma Aubertin-Potter, '"One servant is worth a thousand gadgets": some Oxford College servants 1700–1800', seminar given at All Souls College, Oxford, 3 November 2017

John Bew, *Citizen Clem: A Biography of Attlee* (London, 2016)

L. W. B. Brockliss, Matthew D'Ancona, Robin Darwall-Smith and Andrew Hegarty, '"Everyone of us is a Magdalen Man": The College, 1854–1928', in L. W. Brockliss (ed.), *Magdalen College: A History* (Oxford, 2008)

Thomas Case, *Letters to "The Times" 1884–1922* (Oxford, 1927)

Thomas Charles-Edwards and Julian Reid, *Corpus Christi College, Oxford: A History* (Oxford, 2017)

E. S. Craig and W. M. Gibson (eds.), *Oxford University Roll of Service* (Oxford, 1920)

J. Mordaunt Crook, *Brasenose: The Biography of an Oxford College* (Oxford, 2008)

Judith Curthoys, *The Cardinal's College: Christ Church, Chapter and Verse* (London, 2012)

Ross Davies, *'A Student in Arms': Donald Hankey and Edwardian Society at War* (Abingdon, 2016)

Gerald Gliddon, *VCs of the First World War: Arras and Messines 1917* (2012)

Gerald Gliddon, *VCs of the First World War: Spring Offensive 1918* (2013)

Merve Goddard, Brenda Collins and Mary Hallett, *For God, School & Country: The Upcotts of Christ's Hospital 1902 to 1919* (Netherbury, 2017)

Malcolm Graham, *Oxford in the Great War* (Barnsley, 2014)

G. B. Grundy, *Fifty-Five Years at Oxford: An Unconventional Autobiography* (London, 1945)

Donald Hankey, *A Student in Arms* (17th edn., London, 1917)

Donald Hankey, *Letters of Donald Hankey "A Student in Arms"*, with Notes and an Introduction by Edward Miller, (2nd edn., London, 1919)

Brian Harrison, 'College Life, 1918–1939', in Brian Harrison, *The History of the University of Oxford: Volume VIII: The Twentieth Century* (Oxford, 1994)

Brian Harrison, 'College Servants in Corpus Forty Years Ago', in *The Pelican Record*, Vol. XLV (December 2010)

Brian Harrison (ed.), *Corpuscles: A History of Corpus Christi College, Oxford in the Twentieth Century, Written by Its Members* (Oxford, 1994)

Clare Hopkins, *Trinity: 450 Years of an Oxford College Community* (Oxford, 2005)

P. A. Hunt (comp.) and N. A. Flanagan (ed.), *Corpus Christi College Oxford Biographical Register 1880–1974* (Oxford, 1988)

Ellen N. La Motte, *The Backwash of War: The Human Wreckage of the Battlefields as Witnessed by an American Hospital Nurse* (London, 2014)

Sir Oliver Lodge, *The War and After: Short Chapters on Subjects of Serious Practical Import for the Average Citizen, in A.D. 1915 Onwards* (London, eighth edition 1916, first edition 1915)

John Maddicott, '"An Infinitesimal Part in Armageddon": Exeter College and the First World War', *Exeter College Register* (2017)

Christopher Platt, *The Most Obliging Man in Europe: Life and Times of the Oxford Scout* (London, 1986)

Harold Leslie Rayner, *Letters from France, July 26 1915 to June 30, 1916: Selected by his Mother and printed for private circulation* (London, 1919)

Clare Sherriff, *The Oxford College Barges: Their History, Architecture and Use* (London, 2003)

John Stevenson, 'The College Community, 1905–1950', in Jeremy Catto (ed.), *Oriel College: A History* (Oxford, 2013)

John Stevenson, 'Government, Oxford and Oriel, 1914–1990', in Jeremy Catto (ed.), *Oriel College: A History* (Oxford, 2013)

T. B. Strong, 'The Vice Chancellor's Speech 1914', *Oxford Magazine*, 16 October 1914

Richard Symonds, 'Letters of R. W. Dugdale, 1915–1918', in *Raising the Ladder: Further Worthies and Noteworthies of Corpus Christi College, Oxford* (Oxford, 2008)

J. M. Winter, 'Oxford and the First World War', in Brian Harrison, *The History of the University of Oxford: Volume VIII: The Twentieth Century* (Oxford, 1994)

E. L. Woodward, *Short Journey* (London, 1942)

Websites

P. W. J. Bartrip, 'Vernon, Horace Middleton (1870–1951)', *Oxford Dictionary of National Biography*, Oxford University Press, Sept 2014 <http://www.oxforddnb.com/view/article/106741> (Accessed 20 June 2017)

Commonwealth War Graves Commission website: <http://www.cwgc.org/> (Accessed 26 January 2017)

Bibliography 127

The Illustrated First World War from the archives of *The Illustrated London News*: Food and rationing: <https://www.illustratedfirstworldwar.com/topics/food-and-rationing> (Accessed 17 October 2017)

ACKNOWLEDGEMENTS

Many people, both within Corpus and without, have given invaluable assistance during this project. Professor Sir Brian Harrison offered his support, read through the first draft in its entirety and greatly improved it through his tremendously helpful feedback and suggestions. He, with Julian Reid and Professor Thomas Charles-Edwards, also took enormous trouble to correct the first proofs. In addition, Julian Reid answered many questions and clarified numerous points, and suggested several avenues of interest to explore. Further thanks to Thomas Charles-Edwards for generously providing early access to his twentieth-century chapters of *Corpus Christi College, Oxford: A History*. Joanna Snelling, Julie Blyth and Alice Kelly all kindly read individual chapters, and offered extremely helpful feedback and comments. Dr Kelly also provided assistance during early stages the project, including historiography. Many thanks to Professor Stephen Harrison for providing English translations of Latin memorials; and to Rachel Clifford, Hannah Morgan and Andy Rolfe for answering individual enquiries.

Alex Bostrom, who began this work, generously made his notes and early writings available for use. Local historian Liz Woolley provided invaluable assistance for information on College servants, even undertaking detailed and thorough research across Oxford on the project's behalf. Meanwhile Norma Aubertin-Potter, Clerk to the Archives at All Souls College, kindly shared her own research on College servants. John Stevenson granted early access to his wartime chapters in *Oriel College: A History*. The photography was undertaken by Colin Dunn. Many thanks to the family of J. D. Upcott for allowing us to reproduce his photograph of the Front Quad. The war letters of R. W. Dugdale have been transcribed by the late Mr Roger Wilding; his widow, Mrs Jenny Wilding, kindly gave permission to use extracts from these transcriptions. Information regarding individual Corpuscles was provided by Lesley Wood, Librarian, Archivist and Information Manager at Bedford School; and Caroline Jones, Archivist at Wellington School. Colleagues at The King's School, Worcester, cheerfully granted time and resources. Grateful thanks go to Peter Jones and Patrick Taylor at Profile Books for all their assistance in seeing the project through to publication; and to the care taken by copy editor Rowena Anketell, proofreader Philippa Logan and indexer Elizabeth Wiggans.

I am extremely grateful to my family for reading early drafts of this work and for offering their thoughts; but more especially I wish to thank them for their constant love and support.

APPENDIX

CORPUS CHRISTI COLLEGE
ROLL OF HONOUR

John Duncan Abel (CCC Scholar-elect 1916)
Killed in action 26 March 1918, aged 20

Arthur Addenbrooke (CCC 1901–5)
Died of wounds 5 October 1916, aged 34

Arthur Hugh Aglionby (CCC 1905–8)
Died of wounds 7 November 1918, aged 33

Harry Alexander (CCC 1897–1900)
Killed in action 17 October 1915, aged 36

Godfrey Adolphus Ballard (CCC 1913–14)
Missing, believed killed in action 26 September 1915, aged 20

Arthur Barker (CCC 1910–14)
Died on active service 20 December 1918, aged 27

(George) Hugh Freeland Bartholomew (CCC Commoner-elect 1915)
Died of wounds 2 October 1917, aged 21

Gerald William Beachcroft (CCC 1899–1903)
Killed in action 31 July 1917, aged 36

Major Henry Wynter Blathwayt (CCC 1896–1900)
Killed in action 30 November 1917, aged 40

Tom Lowis Bourdillon (CCC 1906–10)
Killed in action 24 August 1917, aged 29

Gerald Dick Brown (CCC 1905–9)
Missing, believed killed in action 14 April 1918, aged 31

Christopher James Allardyce Buckell (CCC 1909–13)
Killed in action 19 April 1917, aged 26

Christopher Bushell, VC (CCC 1906–9)
Killed in action 8 August 1918, aged 30

Kenneth William Calder (CCC 1912–14)
Died of wounds 21 December 1915, aged 23

The Revd Robert Furley Callaway (CCC 1891–5)
Killed in action 18 September 1916, aged 43

Aidan Chavasse (CCC 1910–14)
Missing, believed killed in action 5 July 1917, aged 25

Roger James Cholmeley (CCC 1890–4)
Died on active service 16 August 1919, aged 47

Eric Fitzgerald Clarke (CCC 1913–14)
Killed in action 9 April 1917, aged 23

Alfred William Clifford (CCC Servant)
Missing, believed killed in action 25 September 1915, aged 21

Arthur Norman Coles (CCC 1910–13)
Killed in action 24 August 1916, aged 24

Harold Arno Connop (CCC Scholar-elect 1917)
Died of wounds 31 March 1918, aged 18

(Henry) Whitaker Coombs (CCC 1911–14)
Died of wounds 2 July 1916, aged 23

Herbert Coupland (CCC 1891–5)
Died on active service in August 1918, aged 45

William Hugh David de Pass (CCC 1911–14)
Missing, believed killed in action 25 March 1918, aged 25

Bertrand Ward Devas (CCC 1901–5)
Killed in action 13 November 1916, aged 34

Robert William Millington Dewhurst (CCC Scholar-elect 1914)
Died of wounds 25 April 1916, aged 20

The Revd Lionel Kenelm Digby (CCC 1902–7)
Killed in action 18 October 1918, aged 34

The Revd Richard William Dugdale (CCC 1908–12)
Killed in action 23 October 1918, aged 28

Harrison Edkins (CCC Charles Oldham Scholar-elect 1915)
Killed in action 15 September 1916, aged 20

Evelyn Arthur Atherley Forrest (CCC 1910–14)
Died of wounds 9 December 1915, aged 23

Charles John Girling (CCC Scholar-elect 1916)
Died of wounds 23 October 1916, aged 19

Barré Herbert Goldie (CCC 1896–1900)
Died of wounds 29 April 1915, aged 38

William Alexander Delap Goodwin (CCC 1912–14)
Killed in action 1 July 1916, aged 23

Richard Aubrey Fuge Grantham (CCC 1914–15)
Killed in action 4 March 1917, aged 21

Reginald Herbert Griffin (CCC 1897–1901)
Died of wounds 7 July 1917, aged 38

Walter Harold Griffiths (CCC Scholar-elect 1914)
Killed in action 30 September 1916, aged 20

William Percival Griffiths (CCC Scholar-elect 1914)
Killed in action 30 March 1915, aged 20

Charles Roderick Haigh (CCC 1907–10)
Killed in action 7 November 1914, aged 26

Arthur John Shirley Hoare Hales (CCC 1900–4)
Killed in action 5 July 1916, aged 34

Donald William Alers Hankey (CCC 1907–10)
Killed in action 12 October 1916, aged 31

William James Henderson (CCC Charles Oldham Scholar-elect 1914)
Killed in action 6 July 1916, aged 20

Arthur Widdrington Herdman (CCC 1905–9)
Killed in action 25 October 1914, aged 28

Reginald Francis Hitchcock (CCC Scholar-elect 1916)
Missing, believed killed in action 14 April 1918, age unknown

John Cyril Holms (CCC 1909–12)
Died of wounds 10 September 1915, aged 23

Malcolm Hutchinson House (CCC Scholar-elect 1916)
Killed in action 3 May 1917, aged 19

Douglas William Hurd (CCC 1913–14)
Killed in action 15 September 1916, aged 20

James Randolph Innes-Hopkins (CCC 1895–8)
Killed in action 24 May 1915, aged 38

James George Gee Janasz (CCC 1912–14)
Killed in action 15 June 1915, aged 22

Sidney Edward James Chippendall Lushington (CCC Commoner-elect 1914)
Died of wounds 25 September 1916, aged 20

Pulteney Malcolm (CCC 1913–14)
Killed in action 25 August 1918, aged 24

Louis Edward Joseph Maude (CCC 1910–14)
Killed in action 1 July 1916, aged 24

Henry Valentine Mills (CCC 1900–4)
Killed in action 25 June 1917, aged 35

Robert Menzies Mocatta (CCC 1911–14)
Killed in action 10 August 1915, aged 23

Henry Morris (CCC 1912–14)
Killed in action 28 September 1915, aged 22

William John Newton (CCC Commoner, matriculated 1879)
Died on active service 16 February 1915, aged 54

Frederick Norris (CCC 1913–15)
Killed in action 7 June 1917, aged 23

John Milner Oliver (CCC 1901–5)
Killed in action 9 July 1916, aged 33

Francis Whitwell Owen (CCC 1913–14)
Killed in action 31 March 1916, aged 21

Alfred Peel (CCC 1914–15)
Killed in action 5 May 1917, aged 22

David Radcliffe (CCC 1913–14)
Killed in action 18 March 1916, aged 21

William Yonge Radcliffe (CCC Commoner-elect 1914)
Died of wounds 19 August 1915, aged 20

Frederick Monro Raikes (CCC 1891–5)
Killed in action 22 February 1917, aged 44

John Francis Raikes (CCC Exhibitioner-elect 1914)
Killed in action 10 October 1916, aged 20

Geoffrey Bury Ramsbotham (CCC 1912–14)
Killed in action 16 May 1915, aged 21

Harold Leslie Rayner (CCC 1909–13)
Killed in action 1 July 1916, aged 26

Harry Esmond Read (CCC 1911–14)
Killed in action 10 August 1917, aged 25

Thistle Robinson (CCC 1911–14)
Killed in action 25 October 1918, aged 26

Mathew Freer Rodger (CCC 1904–7)
Killed in action 23 October 1916, aged 30

Oswald Sidney Royal-Dawson (CCC 1903–7)
Died of wounds 25 August 1917, aged 32

John Henry Raynard Salter (CCC Commoner-elect 1917)
Killed in action 13 October 1917, aged 18

Alexander Morton Shaw (CCC 1906–9)
Killed in action 10 April 1918, aged 30

Anthony Henry Simpson (CCC 1906–10)
Died on active service 1 February 1915, aged 27

Geoffrey Bache Smith (CCC 1913–14)
Died of wounds 3 December 1916, aged 22

Harry Marsden Smith (CCC 1911–14)
Died of wounds 27 February 1917, aged 24

Hugh Stewart Smith (CCC 1908–11)
Killed in action 18 August 1916, aged 27

Stanley Charles Squire (CCC 1912–14)
Killed in action 9 August 1915, aged 22

Cyril Henry Stewart (CCC Scholar-elect 1914)
Killed in action 5 July 1916, aged 20

James Clarke Stokoe (CCC 1912–15)
Killed in action 11 December 1915, aged 22

Andrew John, Viscount Stuart (CCC 1899–1903)
Killed in action 25 September 1915, aged 33

William Louis Tate (CCC 1909–13)
Killed in action 13 March 1915, aged 24

Cuthbert Patmore Taunton (CCC 1913–14)
Killed in action 9 August 1915, aged 20

Alan Graham Thomson (CCC 1900–4)
Missing, believed killed in action 26 September 1917, aged 35

Patrick Grant Thomson (CCC 1914–17)
Died of wounds 29 November 1918, aged 23

Percy Cecil Vaughan (CCC 1897–1901)
Killed in action 25 September 1917, aged 37

Charles Baldwin Dury Wake (CCC Charles Oldham Scholar-elect 1918)
Killed in action 25 September 1918, aged 19

Henry George Ward (CCC Servant appointed 1912)
Killed in action 23 July 1916, aged 17

Reginald Rigden Waters (CCC 1912–14)
Killed in action 24 October 1916, aged 22

Samuel 'Noël' Watts (CCC 1911–14)
Died on active service 28 October 1918, aged 25

Frank Bernard Wearne, VC (CCC 1913–14)
Killed in action 28 June 1917, aged 23

Hugh Wynn Wilding-Jones (CCC 1915–16)
Died of wounds 22 September 1918, aged 22

Percy John Williams (CCC 1913–15)
Died of wounds 17 May 1917, aged 22

George Ouvry William Willink (CCC 1907–11)
Killed in action 28 March 1918, aged 30

George Edward Savill Young (CCC 1902–6)
Died of wounds 31 March 1917, aged 33

INDEX

F

Facer, G. S. (CCC 1919–23) 49
Fellows 68
   on Active Service and Other
      Wartime Work 14–21, 87
   Residing in Corpus 21–5
Fellows Building 2, 70, 78
Final Classical School 94
flu epidemic 1918 50, 74
Flying Corps School 78
food shortages/rationing 82–3, 84
Football 2
Forrest, Evelyn Arthur Atherley (CCC
   1910–14) 132
Foster, Major E. C. 5
'Fourth Centenary Dinner in
   Commemoration of the Founder'
   92
Foxe, Richard 90
freshmen, 'tubbing' 88
Front Quad 78, 82, 99–100, 100
fuel shortages 85
Furse, J. M. H. (sculptor) 96

G

Galsworthy, John
   The Silver Box 36
   Strife 36
gardeners 2, 60, 70
gaudies 73, 86, 91–2
General College Meetings 13, 79, 191
Gentlemen Commoners' Building 65,
   78, 80
Germany 4, 5, 53–4
Gibson, W. M. 107
Girling, Charles John (CCC Scholar-
   elect 1916) 132
Goldie, Barré Herbert (CCC 1896–
   1900) 132
Goldsworthy, J. A. (servant, College
   clerk, Corpus butler) 70

Goodwin, William Alexander Delap
   (CCC 1912–14) 132
Governing Body vii, 5, 7, 8, 9, 13, 22,
   24, 68, 74, 77, 79
Grantham, Richard Aubrey Fuge
   (CCC 1914–15) 132
Greek 5, 87
Greenaway, Officer (St John's Brigade,
   night attendant) 74
Griffin, Reginald Herbert (CCC
   1897–1901) 132
Griffin (servant) 69
Griffiths, Walter Harold (CCC
   Scholar-elect 1914) 132
Griffiths, William Percival (CCC
   Scholar-elect 1914) 7, 27–8, 133
Gropius, E. H. (CCC 1915–20) 49
Grundy, Barbara May 18
Grundy, George Beardoe (CCC
   Fellow 1903–21) 5, 7, 12–13, 16–17,
   20, 21, 86, 94, 95, 97
Grundy, Mabel (née Ord) 16, 17–18
Grundy, Sydney, *A Pair of Spectacles*
   36

H

Haigh, Arthur Elam (CCC Fellow
   1901–5) 101–2
Haigh, (Charles) Roderick (CCC
   1907–10) 101, 102, 133
Haigh Bequest 101
Hale, Sir Edward (CCC 1917–20)
   7, 48–9, 81–2
Hales, Arthur John Shirley Hoare
   (CCC 1900–4) 133
Hall 2, 78–9, 81, 84
   High Table 78, 83, 84
   Junior Commoners' table 81
Hall, C. S. (CCC 1919–20) 49
Hall, Captain Reginald (director of
   Naval Intelligence) 17

Hankey, Donald William Alers (CCC
  1907–10) 28, 35–40, 41, 133
  A Student in Arms 36, 37, 38, 39,
  40, 41
Hargreaves, E. L. (CCC 1919–21)
  49
Harris, Charles Reginald Schiller
  (CCC 1918–20) 49, 82
Harris, Private Robert 83
heating 84–5
Helmdon, living of 25
Henderson, William James (CCC
  Charles Oldham Scholar-elect
  1914) 133
Herdman, Arthur Widdrington (CCC
  1905–9) 133
Herold, J. C. E. (CCC 1914–16,
  1919–20) 49
Herring, E., Report on improving the
  heating apparatus 84
Hertford College 3, 75, 96, 99
Hignett, Charles (CCC 1915–16,
  1918–22) 48, 82
Hitchcock, Reginald Francis (CCC
  Scholar-elect 1916) 133
Hobhouse, R. O. (CCC 1911–14) 7
Holden, Revd O. M. 25
Holms, John Cyril (CCC 1909–12)
  133
Honorary Fellows 92
Hore, Charles (servant) 63
Horn, Walter (director Deutsches
  Entomologisches Museum)
  101
House, Malcolm Hutchinson (CCC
  Scholar-elect 1916) 133
Hunt, E. (servant) 69
Hurd, Douglas William (CCC 1913–
  14) 133
Hussey, D. (CCC 1912–14) 7

I
Incumbents Resignation Act 25
Innes-Hopkins, James Randolph
  (CCC 1895–8) 133
Inspection of the Plate Committee 23

J
Jackson Building 76
Jacobs (Magdalen College jobbing
  bricklayer) 99
Janasz, James George Gee (CCC
  1912–14) 10, 133
Jardine, Major Sir John Eric
  Birdwood (CCC 1909–13) 46
JCR (Junior Common Room) 45, 64
Jesus College 75
Johnson, Major General F. F., CB 78
Jolliffe, Arthur Ernest (CCC Fellow
  1891–1920) 18–19, 20, 22, 86
  Trustee 22
Junior Common Room (JCR) 45, 64
Jurisprudence 2, 23, 24, 106

K
Keble College 6, 75
Ker, William Paton 96
Kitchen 2, 6, 61, 65, 68, 70, 78, 84
Knibbs, Mr (maniciple) 70, 72, 73
Knox, Howard Vincenté (Domestic
  Bursar) 73, 74

L
Lambert, Bertram (CCC Lecturer in
  Chemistry 1909–21) 16
Lambert, Rachel 105
Latin 23, 87
law 2, 4
Lawn Tennis Club 2, 89, 90
League of Nations 100
Lecture Room 3 2, 74, 78, 84, 85
Lecturers 1, 16, 22

W
Wace, R. C. (CCC 1913–14) 7
Wadham College 75
Wahl, Adelbert Emil August (CCC
  1890–2) 46
Wake, Charles Baldwin Dury (CCC
  Charles Oldham Scholar-elect
  1918) 136
Walker, Percy (servant) 63
Walker, R. P. S. (CCC 1919–20) 49
war memorial 59, 60, 95–8
  Memorial Tablet 96
War Office 12, 16, 17, 25, 28, 77, 79,
  80, 82, 87, 99–100
War Service 58
war service decorations 50
War Service Dinner 1920 91–2
Ward, Henry George (servant) 58,
  59–60, 67, 70, 136
Wareham (Rayner's servant) 31, 32
Warren, Edmund Perry (CCC
  Honorary Fellow 1915) 80
Warren, Sir Herbert, President of
  Magdalen College 11
Wasps Dining Club 3, 47, 49, 90
Waters, Reginald Rigden (CCC
  1912–14) 136
Watts, Samuel 'Noël' (CCC 1911–14)
  136
Wearne, Frank Bernard, VC (CCC
  1913–14) 136
Webb, Mr (St John's Brigade) 74
Wells, Wilfred Henry (CCC 1897–
  1900) 46–7

West, P. (servant) 63
Wilding-Jones, Hugh Wynn (CCC
  1915–16) 136
Wilkinson, Geoffrey Herbert (CCC
  1903–7) 46
Williams, Fred E. (servant) 65
Williams, Percy John (CCC 1913–15)
  136
Willink, George Ouvry William (CCC
  1907–11) 10, 20–21, 136
Wills, William Henry (bedmaker)
  66–7
Wilsdon, William (servant, College
  porter) 62, 70
Wilson, John, President 9
women servants, wages 72
women undergraduates 5
Woodcock, Percival (CCC 1919)
  50–51, 74
Woodward, Sir (Ernest) Llewellyn
  (CCC 1908–11, Honorary Fellow
  1960–71) 57
  Short Journey 57
Worcester College 75
Worsley, medical officer 35

Y
Young, Edward Savill (CCC 1902–6)
  137
Young, Joseph (servant) 65–6, 69
Ypres, Menin Gate 27–8, 59